Conversations in Apocalyptic Times

A Guide for the Spiritual Seeker

Robert J. Faas and Arthur Versluis

Apocalypse is revelation of the struggle of light and dark.

Conversations in Apocalyptic Times

This is the best kind of book: it's *useful*. I wish I had read it years ago. Henry Corbin would have loved it—it not only *comes* from the heart but it helps to *activate* it. If you suspect that your life is supposed to be a meaningful journey but you're not sure how to act on that intuition, this wonderful dialogue will help give you direction and courage. It is an open invitation to embark on what Corbin called "a journey toward the Light."

—Tom Cheetham, author of *All the World an Icon, Green Man, Earth Angel*, and many other books.

In an informal, conversational style, the authors offer valuable advice on how one can proceed on the spiritual path. A refreshing antidote to the materialistic and mechanistic view of reality so dominant within the walls of academia.

—Kyriacos Markides, author of *The Magus of Strovolos, Riding with the Lion*, and many other books.

Exciting—whether you agree or not with the ideas in this book, you can benefit from the conversation. It has inspired me.

—Thomas Moore, author of *Care of the Soul*, and *A Religion of One's Own*.

Library of Congress Cataloging-in-Publication Data

Names: Faas, Robert J., author. | Versluis, Arthur, 1959-
author. Title: Conversations in apocalyptic times : a guide for
the spiritual seeker / Robert J. Faas and Arthur Versluis.
Description: Minneapolis, Minnesota : New Cultures Press,
[2021]
Identifiers: LCCN 2020036034 (print) | LCCN 2020036035
(ebook) | ISBN 9781596500372 (trade paperback) | ISBN
9781596500389 (hardcover) | ISBN 9781596500396 (epub)
Subjects: LCSH: Spirituality. | Mysticism.
Classification: LCC BL624 .F33 2021 (print) | LCC BL624
(ebook) | DDC 248--dc23
LC record available at https://lccn.loc.gov/2020036034
LC ebook record available at https://lccn.loc.gov/2020036035

Grailstone Press / New Cultures Press
Minneapolis, Minnesota

Contents

Introduction   1

Beginning the Journey   7

The Turning   29

The Soul's Journey   53

Perennial Truth   87

The Path is Open   111

Preparing for Our Death   139

Your Quest   161

Advice for a Spiritual Seeker   189

INTRODUCTION

This is an unusual book: it is your conversational introduction to a deeper, richer inner life. A collaboration between Robert Faas, a psychologist with a lifetime of counseling experience, now editor of Grailstone Press, and Arthur Versluis, a professor of religion, the book originated in conversations between these two friends over many years, and came into being through audio recordings of thematic conversations over more than a year. In this book, they provide a guide to contemporary and future spiritual seekers, expressed in the accessible and engaging form of a dialogue. So far as we know, this is the only book for general readers to make available practical advice on how to embark on a spiritually transformative inner life journey in this way.

The two speakers bring a wealth of knowledge and life experience to the conversation. Robert Faas, now retired, provided a psychological counseling practice for decades, informed by his deep knowledge of spiritual alchemy, of Christian theosophic mysticism in the tradition of Jacob Böhme, and of Eastern Orthodoxy, in particular, the hesychastic tradition. In addition to his psychology practice, he also guided and still guides a group of spiritual practitioners in the process he discusses here. Arthur Versluis is a professor of religious studies who has published numerous books on mysticism, esoteric religion, consciousness, and related topics, and in addition has trained in a range of secular and Buddhist meditation traditions.

In the contemporary world, there is a surfeit of information, but a dearth of embodied, experiential knowledge. There is scholarship available on all manner of focused subjects, but often it remains at best informational, while disconnected from the larger context of lived experience. This conversational book explores how one can deepen and enrich one's inner life through a wide range of means, all brought together here in the context of a psychologically and spiritually transformative process that involves not just our intellect, but our whole being.

Direct and lucid, the conversational form brings us in, engaging us in the exchange and presenting what for nearly everyone will be a completely new way of understanding the spiritual life. Why is it new? Because in general both historically and certainly in the contemporary world, Christianity became primarily confessional, not understood as a Mystery religion with all that entailed. This Mystery perspective has historically been eclipsed, perhaps never more than in the modern era. But in the understanding developed here, drawing on the classical mystical tradition represented by Dionysius the Areopagite, Meister Eckhart, Jacob Böhme,

Friedrich Schelling, and the hesychastic tradition, its profound dimensions are revealed in a clear way as a psycho-spiritual individual quest, as a movement through our underworld and into the light.

The themes discussed in these conversations are classical ones: the individual quest, of the grail mythos, and of our individual journey to understanding our burdens and woundedness, as well as how we can be healed and not only be illuminated, but illuminate. The conversations ultimately are about darkness and light. And the conversations are permeated by the great works of literature, philosophy, and religion, that is, by the humanities, and by a deep familiarity with those works primarily devoted to helping us understand ourselves not only as we are but also as we can be.

A technological world drives us by externalities, by distraction, and in fact, much of the anxiety and depression of our youth derives from this. People of any age scarcely have time to look inward. Simultaneously, our educational and entertainment apparatus systematically ignore the faint voice of our inner call to a higher and more profound way of life. As a result, you won't find this kind of book, or what it represents in our universities or colleges, nor in our secondary schools. What we are offering here is not to be found in the self-help industry, or in the new age categories, indeed, anywhere else. In fact, this inner path has been very thoroughly eclipsed.

But in this little book, we open a great door, point through it, and let you know that a path beyond that door is there, that it has always been there, and it always will be there for you. Why? Because an expression of truth, by virtue of being true, existed in the archaic past, exists now, and will exist in the future. That is the very nature of what is true, for it is both within and beyond time. This is a little book about the Mysteries we can experience as humans, and about how you can embark on a quest to understand them yourself.

It is a book about both the darkness and the light. As Jacob Böhme so clearly saw, in this human life we can give ourselves over to wrathful and destructive energies, or we can begin to transform those energies through the Christic path into strength and loving kindness. It is not enough to imagine that a new age is somehow upon us, or soon will be upon us. To engage in a spiritual process of alchemical transmutation, we have to look unflinchingly at how we've gone astray and at the burdens and wounds we bear, but we also will move through our own underworld on our quest for healing and light.

This might be a disquieting book for you in places. It might express ideas or advice or observations you've never heard before. What we'd ask is that you be with what we say, and reflect on it without immediately judging it. Perhaps, like a seed, it will take root and grow. If not, that's all right. If the book isn't speaking to you, it might not be meant for you at this time. Let it go for now, and when you come back, perhaps you'll see it in a different light. But if it does speak to you, if in it or through it you hear the call to this mysterious journey, the quest at the very heart of what it means to be human, we wish you godspeed on your path. After all, it was meant for you.

—Robert Faas and Arthur Versluis

CHAPTER ONE

Beginning the Journey

Robert Faas (RF), Arthur Versluis (AV)

AV: I'm sitting in the library of Robert Faas, and we're talking about Schelling, and various metaphysical and spiritual topics. I thought that at the beginning of our conversation we might reflect, for a little bit, on what advice we might have for someone who is not familiar with the kinds of things that you find in a library, a really great library like this. What advice would we have for someone who is seeking, who is recognizing that something is not quite right in the society that we're in? Who perhaps has gone through some kind of educational institution, came out the other side, and recognized that a lot of things seemed to be missing. And wondered perhaps what those things were. What advice would you have for somebody who's really beginning and investigating for the first time, looking for more meaning in life?

RF: I would suggest two things: one is to be quiet. Silence. Begin to seek out more quiet in your life. If you want to begin on a quest, one of the most detrimental things right now, to any form of inner quest, is the amount of noise and constant distraction that goes on. I'd begin by suggesting that people establish a zone of silence and quiet for themselves. Which would be preparation for the soul to go deeper. And I think the other would be to seek out some of the mystery in things that still exist beneath the surface, but again in modern society we've pretty much lost the element of mystery. Technology, all the modern things, really don't speak at all to the mystery of the human being, or the mystery of existence, or spiritual mystery. Beginning means seeking for things that are beyond the everyday.

AV: I would add to that. I think both of those are absolutely true. Many of the students I see and work with, and I myself for that matter, we're all immersed in technology. We're trapped by technology that distracts us and keeps us occupied at a superficial level. And that in itself provides stimulation and it provides a reward for stimulation, which is more stimulation. Leaving that behind, at least for a time now and then, and having a time during the day when you don't have that around. I would suggest keeping your technology, at least part of the time, on mute. Have it so it doesn't bark at you all the time. Another thing I would suggest, and this ties in with both of the things you were talking about, is finding time to be in nature. Increasingly, because we live in technological bubbles, we're not in the natural world. We're in an artificial world. It's a world, to some extent, also of our own superficial, materialistic consciousness. It exists on a materialistic level that is really superficial and that is really based in a kind of stimulus-response kind of relationship with other people, with things. Whereas being in nature has meaning as well. It is a place where you can discover meaning in a primordial way. Meaning comes out of a context, and part of our contextualization, as human beings, requires silence. And it requires nature, the natural world, untamed mountains, valleys, the ocean. It's in that kind of context that we can begin to discover meaning in a deeper way. You were using the term "quest," and that's not accidental. I wonder if you might talk a little more about thinking of life as a quest, and as an inner quest?

RF: Yes, you're right, it's not accidental. I really believe that humanity is meant to be on a quest, a spiritual quest, a quest regarding our existence, in order to really deepen our existence. And that the whole idea of a quest was much more prominent, even in the more recent past. But, like a lot of things, it's just not spoken of very much these days. No matter what religions you look at, the fact is that a quest is so important, is really central to religion. And I think, especially in Christianity, the quest of the individual soul had enormous meaning and probably the most meaning of all in terms of one's destiny. So to no longer be questing, in a sense, is much like a death. And it turns one over to whatever forces that are there as a kind of a plaything. Because a quest helps to establish a ground.

AV: There's a journey, and it has a purpose, which is discovering meaning, and it's a journey, which means a movement through time and space. And that's very much part of the grail cycle and the grail tradition, which plays an important role in Western European culture, although it's not widely discussed now. Maybe you could talk a little bit about quest in terms of the grail and in terms of grail mythology and that tradition and the role that it plays.

RF: I think it's certainly true that the idea of a quest, and the grail quest, is at the center of both Eastern and Western Christianity. Jung talked about these things a lot, especially that the soul is meant to undergo a quest. And in Christianity, the quest often had something to do with the process of divinization, theosis or regeneration, rebirth, and then gradually began to, more and more, go into the time of the grail. In a way, the whole purpose is to undertake the quest, which would point to, ultimately, again, one's regeneration and the process of what you must do in order to successfully complete the quest. And to say "the grail" was really another way of referring to the Risen Christ and the light. The quest has to do with the light. And to follow that meant everything.

AV: How does the grail correspond to the light? How do you see that connection? The grail mythos and light, how does that appear?

RF: I think that especially in the descriptions and the imagery of the vessel, the cup, you know it's always a shining, a very spiritual vessel connected to both light and substance. So it has to do with the brilliance of the light, which brings both clarity and undergoing a process of what we would term a refining process many times. This is the process in which we have to go through the death of our ego-self, and allow that to happen. What sustains us, in that, is the light. And here we're talking about the Christ as the risen light, especially in the grail. Someone, or something, beyond the self has to be able to take one through the journey. Fundamentally, the journey means the giving up of the old self, in order that one undergoes the necessary changes for a new or regenerate self to become birthed.

AV: So for someone who is coming out of a contemporary environment where many of these things are unfamiliar, still, there's probably a sense of recognition of what you're talking about that stirs or awakens for some people, someone listening to this or reading this, someone hears it or reads it and thinks, "yes, I understand what it means, what you're referring to, about a quest and also about leaving behind the old self and ego and moving toward and realizing what's beyond that. What's beyond 'self.'" That's a way of expressing in universal terms what manifests in particular ways in stories and myths and a particularly pure form of it is the grail mythology. But what more would you have to say about the experience of leaving behind the old self or the ego in context of contemporary society, where it's not an environment conducive necessarily to the kind of quest that we're talking about? In some sense what we're talking about is a sort of a counter-cultural or a counter-societal kind of movement, in that it goes beyond what we normally take for granted. And one of the things that I don't see in the academic or the educational world is recognition of myth or emphasis on any kind of quest, or for that matter in the departments of literature, an emphasis on literature as a quest or of literature as having greater meaning or higher meaning beyond just entertainment value or intellectual gymnastics. So what I would wonder is as someone is thinking about embarking on a quest, what would be some literature, what would be some mythology or some sources, what would be a place to go to find footing, to find a kind of a map, you could say? I think we have different kinds of maps, different kinds of options for the quest. I suppose we could divide them up roughly. There's classical literature, there's Mystery literature, and there's mystical literature, there are alchemical writings, and then something that we're both particularly drawn to, the tradition of Christian theosophy, which draws together many of these different strands into a single strand, making it challenging. What would you suggest for someone who's starting out looking at all of this different literature, but looking at it for meaning and looking at it for a source to help guide us? What would you suggest as sources among these different currents that we're talking about?

RF: I think that all of the currents that you named would be very helpful, and what I would focus on in these currents, is finding the ones in which there is a journey through the underworld. That's what I would see as the key or the thread to focus on the myths, the writings that have to do with a journey of the underworld. I think, in modern society especially, there's really nowhere to journey. I mean older civilizations and peoples and mystics and writers knew you had to go through the underworld, you know? Your own inner underworld and make that descent, that catabasis, before you could really go anywhere or develop anything. So, what I would look for in Greek myths, Christian works, any of the great works, is focusing on the underworld journey. That would really be the key to setting one in the right direction.

AV: You use the word "Mystery," and I want to come back to that because I think it's critical. But the word "Mystery" in English harks back to these mysterious traditions of great antiquity and antiquity and then late antiquity, called the "Mysteries." And the Mystery traditions... no one is fully certain what went on there because initiates were sworn to secrecy and kept it. But there are some hints or indications. I think I can safely say I've read all of the literature available on the Mysteries. The Mysteries were initiatory traditions in which people would go into a night setting and, in a group, experience a movement through the underworld, through darkness, into illumination. And it was said that the sun shone at midnight, and that the light shone in the darkness. That's a Mystery tradition that pretty closely reflects what you're talking about. So the Mysteries themselves, whether it's the Eleusinian Mysteries, whether it's the Samothracian Mysteries, or in other locations—because there were a number of Mystery locations—all did in fact involve a movement through the underworld, or a symbolic underworld journey, and then illumination. So that's actually the essence of what the Mysteries were, when we go back to the origin of the word "Mysteries," and that's one of the things that seems to be missing in our modern world. So I wondered what would you have to say about Mystery? How we can nonetheless have Mystery *in* the modern world?

RF: I think, certainly, it's quite true that Mystery is missing. The long tradition of Mystery has really become obscured and I think that in a special way, Christianity used to be more imbued in the early centuries with being a Mystery tradition, but more in terms of existence itself, which in early Christianity *was* the undergoing of Mystery. By that I mean, one of the ways where Christianity had gradually gone off course from its earlier times was not understanding the descent of Christ into Hades. That there was something new in the whole Christian Mystery tradition that happened there. Which is still accessible, which is why I think it's still so important for today. What was new there, in regards to the Mystery, was that in Christ's descent into Hades, Christ changed the nature of the underworld. It was no longer the same as it was before that. So one of the most significant aspects of all history was a descent, which wasn't just a descent into the underworld but changed the nature of the underworld into something that it had never been before. Which was primarily by bringing his light and binding the powers of darkness in the underworld, the souls were granted the ability to no longer be bound to not evolving into a higher state and could enter into the higher light world, or what one would often call the heaven realm. So Christ brought in the light that had the power and the energy to give to the souls, enabling them to undergo the mystery of metamorphosis into a higher state. And in that realm, that was of course the major change in the Mysteries. The original Mysteries became "old Mysteries" and Christianity revealed the "new Mysteries." And that was not very deeply understood, as Christianity of course became more theologically bound, and politicized. In this process, the loss of the Christic Mystery tradition, especially in regard to the underworld and the process of regeneration was really not understood very well, and is still not understood very well. So I think that the access that you have through the light of Christ in that regard reveals much more of an open door to the whole Mystery tradition, especially to the modern person. The accessibility to the Light has changed.

AV: Essentially what you're describing is Christianity understood as a Mystery tradition, as Mystery revelation. And that's, for most people I think, a very unfamiliar way of understanding that tradition. For most people, what they're exposed to in terms of Christianity may be a kind of fundamentalist form of it, which tends to be very literalistic. They might have been exposed to anti-materialist, scientific, or atheist perspectives that are also very literalistic. I think it's very widespread as a world view, materialism.

RF: Yes. Very powerful.

AV: It is very powerful, and it takes many different forms. It takes not only the atheist, overtly materialistic, anti-religious form, but it also takes the religious forms of extreme fundamentalisms of different kinds, these ISIS people, or other fanatical groups with different perspectives. They are all materialistic at core, and they share, even though they're at each other's throats, in reality they share much in common in terms of perspective. In that, for many of them, perhaps the vast majority of them, a Mystery tradition and the idea of life as a quest and of revelation of light and Christ's light is a completely different way of understanding Christianity, in particular. And so, I can understand why this being all relatively unfamiliar, it's not totally clear where someone would go with it. Where would they go, what they would do next having discovered that although what they thought was Christianity does exist, that's not the only form? There are other kinds, and other ways of understanding it and also practicing it. What would you suggest for someone in terms of an initial kind of approach and practice? Within this tradition, where might they go? Orthodoxy provides something different than Catholicism and Protestantism. My own experience in an Orthodox church, specifically we're talking about Greek Orthodox in this case, is that the liturgy has something almost like an electrical current, something indescribable that is present there that was not familiar in my own Protestant Calvinist upbringing. Now I'm not suggesting necessarily that someone run out and convert, but I am saying what would be some good next steps if you're thinking about where to go or what practices to undertake?

RF: That presents its own difficulties. Because where is a good starting point for this in these times? I mean you certainly could, as you suggest, for some people, go to Eastern Christianity where there is much more of a preservation of a mystical and Mystery sacramental tradition. In fact, the words "Mystery" and "Sacrament" mean the same thing. And still in Eastern Christianity, there is still the idea of the Mysteries of the sacrament. So that type of tradition could be a great deal of help to someone. It's almost as if the question has to be answered in a way in which for some people, going to church is a good starting place to begin the journey to go deeper. For others, the idea of becoming part of a church or an institution is not going to be their way. I think that there has to be a multiple answer to that question. For the person alone, for the person who would like to have a community, these would be different paths. But I think that at the core, the same thing on the path would be that one begins to open oneself to the Risen Christ. In other words, thinking about this in a somewhat different way all things point, and scripture ends, with the Risen Christ. The Risen Christ is ultimately the reality that has survived in presence for everyone. In other words, whether you're a member of a church or whatever it might be, there is a spiritual presence that the Risen Christ, the risen Light can bring to any individual. So, in a sense, you can start with Christ saying "I am with you always." That the knowledge that there is a reality of being with, in a kind of a sacred dialogue way, no matter if you go through a church, if you do not, no matter what path you take there is someone, in this person in this divine presence, the divine light that you can start with. So I think that that's what, at the core, no matter where you would like to start, you don't have to start alone. That I think is a fundamental element to this.

AV: I would say that I certainly understand what you're alluding to, because it is natural for one to think that the beginning of the quest might be in some kind of religious or institutional circumstance, and it's true that it might, but I remember in my own family's church there was a middle-aged minister who was given a chance to preach one summer. In his sermon, he referred to the great mystic Meister Eckhart, probably the greatest mystic in the entire German tradition. In many respects, he and Böhme together are the, you know one in Catholicism and one in Protestantism, together are without doubt the greatest. He referred to Eckhart, and he referred to his own mystical experience and he was almost fired from the church and he was not allowed to preach in the summer again. I mention that because on the one hand, of course, you have institutional hostility towards what we're talking about, which has manifested very directly, in that case. That's one thing. But the other is that the mystical tradition does exist. And it exists regardless of the institutional structure, and separately from it because what we're talking about is not constrained by artificial barriers. What we're talking about is something that is our own natural inheritance. It is ours if we seek it. And the first step is really recognizing that something exists. Because you can't really look for it very well if you can't see it exists. We have an intuition that what we're alluding to here exists, but now in this conversation we're actually pointing it out. Here I want to add that there actually is a fairly extensive textual tradition— it's not huge, but it certainly exists— that supports what you're talking about in terms of a mystical tradition. That is, there are other mystical traditions outside of Christianity, of course. What we're talking about is Christianity, and within that tradition there are sources to refer to. And if I were going to point to any of them, great though Eckhart is, and Tauler, and Ruysbroek, all of whom are great—

RF: John of the Cross.

AV: John of the Cross, that's true.

RF: Hildegard of Bingen, I mean there are a number. Yes.

AV: Right. But I would suggest, very straightfor-
wardly, a place to go is Dionysius the Areopagite, because his are very short works.
They're very pure, in that they're a source for
both Eastern and for Western Christianity. And
Dionysius the Areopagite has treatises about the
nature of what later is termed "unknowing."
Which is knowing what transcends our limited
self, our limited awareness, and also he has
writings on what he refers to as the celestial hierarchy. The different stages of moving upward,
closer to the divine. And so if I were going to say
"go to one Ur-source," early in the Christian tradition, to get a sense of Christianity as Mystery
that's common both to East and West, the brief
writings of Dionysius the Areopagite are one
place that I would recommend, because so
much that is important is there, in his work.
Those would be some thoughts both about what
is sometimes helpful institutionally but often
harmful, and about going back to the Ur-source
of the whole mystical tradition, both East and
West. It's not the only source, obviously there
are other places to look, but that's one that I
would recommend. What would you add to
that?

RF: Just that Dionysius certainly is one of the
mountains, and I think it would be a great help
to read as much as one could in his works to get
that sense of mystery and mystical flavor, espe-

cially in relationship to the light and to Christ. The tradition in the East that would help a person is the hesychastic one. Which, as you know, is a Greek word for quiet, silence, stillness, and, of course, having to do with the centrality of light. In both East and West, quiet and light, and reading in those kinds of traditions I think can bring a person into a realization that this is what the quest might look like. That it has to do with the deeper things of the light, and that opens up the question: how am I able, on my own level, to prepare myself for the coming of the light? What can I do beyond reading, which I believe helps prepare the mind? What must I do? And I think here we get into a part that is not talked about a lot, but we have to look at the burdens we carry. If one would like to rise, it's not going to be very possible if one is being weighed down by a great many burdens. Which is really the human condition. I mean, who does not have their burdens from the past? Things going on in their life? We can almost say by definition that all people are carrying their own burdens. And to begin to understand that okay, these burdens are some of the things that I'm carrying that I have to become free from. So I think that we enter into the existential question that if I'm going to go on the quest, how can I go on the quest if I'm really burdened down? And beginning to start with what are my personal burdens? In other words, we have to take a look at ourselves in kind of caring, open way, just starting to see where have I come to? What have I been through? What have I gone through? So in a sense it's kind of a psychological, but of course also spiritual question. At heart, what we're dealing with is both the psychological and the spiritual, and we can't ignore our own psychology or our own spirituality. So it's like ancient wisdom again, we start with ourselves. What have I become up to this point?

AV: And where do I want to go? What do I want to become? Because the very term *theosis* suggests becoming more, realizing what is beyond us in our more limited capacity. That more is possible to us.

RF: Yes. Yes and that very term implies another, the term "deification." The whole idea of the quest is a potentialization, an absolute potentialization of the human condition. A raising up is absolutely intrinsic. If we naturally have these burdens, if we're going to be raised up, what must we do with the burdens? And that in fact we have to start with our burdens where we are. Which is what a good alchemist, a spiritual alchemist would say, as well as many others. That we begin by seeing who I am, in a sense mirroring oneself up to this point in time.

AV: And as the hero or heroine in a mythological cycle, if we want to think of ourselves that way, setting out on a journey. The very word "burden" also suggests laying down. Because a burden is something you carry, and at some point you lay it down in order to be able to move on the journey, because otherwise you're so burdened that you can't move. And so a journey requires some, at least some degree of freedom. Freedom to move, that is. Freedom to go on the journey. And then there's the question of where one is going, and we've talked about that to some extent when you referred to the journey as being both psychological and spiritual. I think that's a perspective that isn't always recognized, I think it's often common to have interpretations that are either one or the other. So the journey is psychological, but it has spiritual dimensions—

RF: I think you're absolutely right there. You have people from both sides, those with spirituality saying what do I have to do with psychology, and those who have a lot of psychology saying what do I have to do with spirituality? And so it's usually unfortunately kind of divided, like they're separate.

AV: That's right. But here, what you're suggesting is that they're actually integral. That they're directly related to each other and that by implication a spiritual journey also requires psychological journeying. And that's something that I would like to explore in our next conversation because I think there are some things that I can see moving forward that we would need to discuss. And some of those have to do with the journey through the underworld, it has to do with darkness.

RF: Yes, absolutely.

AV: It has to do with the nature of evil, with the nature of our own shadows, and how to work with that. And that's too much to try to cover in just an introductory conversation, but I could see that it's coming up, that it's part of this. And so, I hope that you'll join us in the next conversation in which we move from the beginning of the journey, where one is, where one is lost, or confused in a modern educational system that doesn't offer anything like a sense of mystery or invite us to silence or beginning a quest, so this is extra-institutional. This is something outside any kind of system. Including educational, but for that matter religious or even psychological systems, or any kind of system—

RF: Political.

AV: Political.

RF: Especially. In other words, yes. It is outside systems.

AV: That's right. What we're talking about is what Jung called individuation. Now I'm not a Jungian, so it's not that I'm invoking Jung to invoke Jungianism, but rather that he's right. That in the heart of what we're talking about, not all of what we're talking about but part of what we're talking about, is in fact coming to know who we are. And coming to know ourselves, and coming to know the nature of the world in a deeper way. And that's something Jung referred to as individuation and it is not Jungian, it's not psychological, it's not political, it is something else that we have to work through on our own and that has to do with our dreams, that has to do with our inner life, it has to do with coming to understand who we are and what the nature of our own meaning is. What meaning itself really is. Because what we've been told, what we've been given is not sufficient. And we know that. If you've listened this far, or if you've read this far, then you already intuitively feel that. And so what we're going to do in our next conversation I think is begin to explore the hard topics of dealing with the shadow, of dealing with darkness, what you might encounter in the underworld, what the underworld means in this context, and so look forward to the next conversation.

RF: Yes, I do as well. In a very real way I think what it takes us into is process. Theosis, regeneration, rebirth, whether east or west, all that means that there is a process that one has to undergo. And that's where, in a way that we've come to, that we have to explore what that process looks like. The process starts with oneself.

AV: The process starts with oneself, and understanding one's burdens, and understanding the nature of the journey.

RF: One's history. Psychological history. I mean, just yes. All of those things.

AV: So, the next conversation will be what the process is and how that intersects with these themes of darkness and the unconscious and shadow. I look forward to it.

RF: I do as well.

CHAPTER TWO

The Turning

Robert Faas (RF), Arthur Versluis (AV)

AV: We might start by reflecting a little on the last conversation, because we were thinking aloud about what sort of advice we'd give to someone setting out on an exploration of the inner life. When we ended, we suggested the next conversation would continue the discussion by looking at the process. The process, a quest or journey, begins by recognizing the burdens that we bear. We come to understand more deeply the nature of the shadow and working through darkness and the dark night of the soul. What would you have to say to someone who's begun to engage in the process of the inner life and has started to begin to come to terms with the shadow? Or maybe another way to put it is if you have come to some sort of purgatory in your life: what kind of advice would you give to someone like that?

RF: My advice is fundamentally about coming to understand the contrarium of your soul. In other words, understanding that our soul is a contrarium of light and dark. And that what's developed in us is both of those elements. So to begin by acquainting oneself with the standpoint of, "All right, I'm a contrarium. I'm not just one way, but I do exist in a contrarium," so it's about one getting acquainted with one's own contrarium. I think that is clarified by Gretchen [Faas's] article on coming to terms with the dying process through mirroring what is happening in the soul. In a way, it's about going forward, because that article was about the process of mirroring the soul and that if we do that, we have a natural archetypical process of the soul in which the soul wants to review itself. The review is from the standpoint of what's always been important to the soul and from a moral standpoint, basically the "how I lived my life" standpoint and what kind of decisions have shaped me, and what has brought me to my overall present state.

AV: What you're referring to is mirroring the soul, becoming conscious and becoming aware of who we are in review, looking at who we are and how we've come to where we are, and sometimes where we're at could be a kind of inflection point or, you know, even a kind of crisis point. I'll give you an example of that. I was contacted, very recently, by someone, something that happens on a fairly regular basis because

I'm a somewhat public figure as a professor, and my contact information is out there. I was contacted by a woman who has gone through, essentially, a kind of crisis. I don't know her, but I do know what she's describing and if I don't want to go into a lot of details but one of the things she wrote, which I thought was germane to what we are talking about is that she said "because of some of the things which happened, I feel I have a hole in my soul." She was essentially reaching out and I responded and said "I think I can help. I'm not sure, but why don't you give me a little bit more, in terms of information and your background?" So that's something that actually happening right now. I wondered, what your thoughts are about that? Here we're talking about someone who is engaged in a soul review, but in the context of what she feels is really an inflection point. Really it's something akin to a crisis.

RF: Yes, that makes eminent sense. When you were saying "crisis," I will always prefer that to the original Greek word that often gets translated as "judgment." But what is the word really saying? The Greek word really is *krisis*, but it doesn't mean specifically judgment, it means more the soul coming into conflict, confronting these light and dark aspects. It's more a weighing than a judgment, a weighing out. I think that when we are in crisis, there is a weighing out that's happening. We're learning to change with the soul. We've gone through traumatic things or we're coming to a point where maybe we've been going down the wrong track and need to change, and we're sensing that, but we're in crisis, so to speak. For very good reason this can be used, this point of reflection, as a way of undertaking a true turning, a regeneration.

AV: And in her case, one of the things I would ask is: is this a domain of psychology alone? If she were to go to a psychologist whose goal is "existential" or adjusting to society or adjustment—sometimes people will use this word "adjustment"—is that alone really enough? What's the relationship between psychology and spirituality, in terms of someone, in this case it's someone who to my thinking is in a spiritual crisis? I don't know her— it could also be a psychological crisis. To what extent does contemporary psychology offer benefit to someone who's actually also in a spiritual crisis? What would you have to say about that?

RF: I think for the individual, unfortunately, there's a great problem there. Because modern psychology doesn't really recognize the spiritual. Just like many modern people with regard to religion, some people don't recognize anything to do with psychology. So I think we have a terrible kind of misunderstanding between the psyche and the spirit, spiritual and psychological. They're not the same domain, but we are in both and we need both. As you were saying about just bringing someone back into, and adjusting to society that has already lost control isn't really, ultimately, going to help a person. There are those who certainly need to be able to make an adjustment so they can handle going forward, but that's all. We [in psychology] kind of lost the purpose, here.

AV: That's right. And in the case of this young woman, it could be that, in the kind of struggle that she feels and that she's expressing, she goes to a psychiatrist or to a psychologist who in turn can offer her, in some cases, a pharmaceutical remedy of some kind. So she might be offered some kind of antidepressant, which dulls or buoys her in some sense but doesn't really address the really deeper, spiritual dimensions that are clearly there, or what's really going on. And so I'm not going to discount the benefit of those things in all cases, I think there are cases where it's called for, but here I'm asking really what is a path forward for someone like that? Because she, in going to a contemporary psychologist, probably is going to be given some advice, some basis for moving forward, but she's not going to be with someone whose worldview includes spiritual dimensions. So how do you integrate those two aspects? Because the psychological is part of what we're talking about. How can she move forward? What should she do?

RF: I think it's possible for her to find someone who does combine both, in other words, psychosynthesis. There are practitioners that use psychology and spirituality that are in union, and maybe first of all looking for someone who actually, even though they might not always be easy to find of course, but who walks both paths and their practice includes both psychological and spiritual therapeutic ways and understanding. If you can't find some one individual like that, I'd even say get a psychologist to help with some of the psychological and maybe a minister, priest, or someone who has skills or expertise in the psychospiritual and the spiritual side of things. Really talking to people who represent both sides of this reality.

AV: That's good advice, and I'm going to pass that along. In the meantime, if we return back to the idea of soul review and looking at the *contrarium*, what is the path of integration that you're talking about here? What's the process? Here you're talking about a solitary process that's not a process with someone else, but looking at your own inner life and reviewing that, what's the next step beyond that?

RF: First, a very critical point inherent in what we were talking about but needs to be brought forth is that who or what is the mirror? And the mirror really is the Light. And that is in the person of the Risen Christ. One needs to not, in a sense, do one's own analysis, although certainly that would be helpful, but be able to open to the light of Christ in oneself and allow that light to mirror back to the person, to stare into the state of his or her *contrarium*. So that one does need to, even in the mirroring process of course, begin the process of letting go and opening to something, someone beyond the self. And allowing that divine presence, that light presence of Christ, to begin to help with the process of mirroring.

AV: What we're talking about here has psychological dimensions in that you're referring to burdens, past traumas or past difficulties, and to positive things, positive and negative both, in reviewing. So there is to some extent a psychological connection, but the spiritual dimension, the transformative one, comes through the light of Christ.

RF: Actually, both of them. I think Christ illuminates both the psychological and the spiritual dimension. In other words, there's not that division of the psychological or the spiritual, it's the psycho-spiritual reality of the soul. We shouldn't ignore the psyche or our spirit. We are both, we are not just psyches. We have a spirit. Even in the old descriptions we're body, soul, and spirit. Of course, the spirit has taken a bit of a rough ride nowadays, meaning that so much of the nature of the spirit has been lost. But we need to realize that we are still creatures of the soul and spirit. And both of those dimensions both have to be reckoned with. It would certainly be a rare person that is totally a psychological person, or a rare person that is totally a spiritual person. We're engaging psycho-spiritually all the time, even though in a way we're delving more into it in what we're talking about. What Christ did was bring healing and light into the split between the soul and spirit, the individual soulish spirit, really encompassing both.

AV: What role does the harrowing of hell play in what you're talking about? People might not be familiar with the term "harrowing of hell" but perhaps you could talk a little bit about that and what role that plays because engaging in a quest, which is what we started by talking about, a quest doesn't include only include going out toward a particular goal without encountering any obstacles or any difficulties or any suffering. Quite the opposite: in the journey, in classical myths, the hero or heroine, or both, are beset by enemies or dangers and have to confront fear. That's part of the very nature of the quest or the journey which is a kind of testing, and I wonder how you would connect what I'm referring to here.

RF: Such an important moment. I would refer to the way Eastern Christianity has discussed it, having much more to do with the harrowing of hell, even though certainly the West used to have a similar understanding at one time, this harrowing was quite important to humanity and to Christianity. I think one of the best ways might be to understand, what did Christ do in the harrowing of hell? I think one of the major figures is the great Christian mystic Jacob Böhme, who talked about Christ in the underworld, as well as one of his followers, Dionysius Andreas Freher, who had a long treatise about what Christ did in the underworld and how Christ entered the underworld. Which was principally that Christ entered the underworld with soul and spirit, so now we have both soul and spirit and his own inner body of light. He, with this triumphant being of light, Christ gave up the body and then entered the underworld. This was in triumph. This was in overcoming. So Christ, the light-body, soul, and spirit, primordial reality, overcame the darkness and with divine power brought to the souls of humanity a new dispensation of being able to go further and bringing them the light in the darkness so that their souls could undertake the journey of further purification and reaching up to the state of transfiguration, which would allow the soul to enter into the inner light world, which we call "heaven." But this (the underworld) would now be the place that undergoing this transfiguration process took place. Making it possible for those souls to undergo that journey. Which I think is directly applicable to the whole idea that the therapeutic reality the soul needs is the idea of Christ being the light and bringing the light into the underworld. He truly brought it so that one may be able to cleanse and account for waywardness and on the other side heal the wounds that the soul is carrying. So you have this psychospiritual therapeutic process on the other side.

AV: It's very much prefigured by and akin to the ancient Mystery traditions of Europe, which were all about entering into the underworld. The Mysteries took place at night, there were alarming or frightening apparitions, there was a period of separation, of loss, and then rediscovering, reuniting, and illumination. That's a kind of very brief summary, a thumbnail sketch of what we know of the Mysteries of Isis, the Mysteries at Samothrace, the Mysteries at Eleusis, and in all of those you had the same descent into the underworld. That descent is symbolic, but in the Mysteries, in what accounts we have, or what references we have, it was also very real. So it's a combination of symbolic and real. It's not that the Mysteries were only symbolic and people sat there as if they were in a movie theater, but rather they were transformative. And that's exactly what we're talking about here as well. Essentially what you're describing is Christianity understood as a Mystery tradition. And here I'm referring to Mystery with a capital M. Christianity understood as a Mystery, as a salvific Mystery tradition. And that's of course very different than what most people would be familiar with in terms of understanding Christianity.

RF: Yes, that so much of that is visible in the early mystics as well as the great Christian poets and writers, certainly, and some of the early Church Fathers. So this has always been there, and you're absolutely right, it's almost nonexistent in contemporary culture. This ancient understanding isn't being passed on. And so we have, almost the most central question of all is, what did Christ do when you're talking about the Mysteries? What did Christ bring into the underworld that was different than what the earlier Mysteries had been able to do? It's really quite a central question because something changed in the very nature of the underworld. Christ's descent was not like an Orpheus or others who have descended and then in a sense came back— Christ overcame. That reality is often not considered at all. It wasn't just a pivot to the underworld, it was an overcoming and a changing of its nature forever. Interestingly enough, I was reading something that I thought we might get into. It's by Philip Sherrard, and it's an article he wrote on Simeon the Theologian and he actually addresses some of this. He says, "but for all their similarities, there were big differences between the Pagan Mysteries and the Christian Mysteries." The god of the Mystery religion was not an active god, he was a passive god. There might be a movement of man towards him, he might allow man in moments of rapture to take possession of him, but he himself did not move towards man. He did not, himself, actively love man. There was no *philanthropia*. Second, in Christianity there was a new attitude towards suffering. The pre-Christian attitude towards suffering was likewise a path to a negative attitude. In the Pagan religion, man had to suffer. And now, suffering, maybe he would learn some wisdom. But Christ's attitude was the opposite of the Greek hero. He gave the myth of the wounded and dying god a new significance. Christ by his own choice entered into suffering on the way to spiritual fulfillment. Suffering, for him, was something positive. What was pain and distress in this world is for the spirit the best way to liberation. The divinity himself cannot think it unworthy to go through the shamefulness of death. So the mystery of the Mystery religion was taken further by Christ. In other words, this Mystery of fulfillment was a kind of new dispensation in terms of the meaning of suffering. What are your reactions to those passages?

AV: There are a couple of things that I would say. One is you're drawing on Philip Sherrard, who is of course such a beautiful writer; he expresses things with such clarity and precision and beauty. In this vision, or understanding, the ancient Mysteries and the Pagan traditions are not seen as in opposition to Christianity but in relation to it. So as a result there isn't the kind of polemical opposition that has so bedeviled Christianity, and instead what you have is continuity and fulfillment, and as a result one sees something very similar to this, and we've talked about this before, in Ireland there's actually a deep continuity between the ancient Pagan traditions, some of which were almost certainly akin to what we know of the ancient Mysteries, and Christianity. Celtic Christianity was very akin to the perspective that you're describing, wherein instead of being a kind of narrow and purely belief-centered kind of doctrinal position—and of course it has doctrines, not saying it doesn't—Christianity becomes a much fuller, all-embracing or all-incorporating Mystery tradition. The way is then opened for a process, for us to undergo a process ourselves as opposed to simply asserting belief, and there's a big difference between the two. So that process is metaphysically dependent on the harrowing of hell and Christ transforming the underworld. That transforming the underworld is necessary in order to comprehend that what we're talking about is a spiritual process that we undergo, not simply acquiescence in a particular set of points that are seen as opposed, somehow, to everything that went before. A transformative or a transfigurative process is really very different, and that's what you're describing. And man has a metaphysical foundation, a metaphysical basis.

RF: Yes. Exactly what comes into my mind is metaphysical, that this is a continuity of mystery. In other words, Christianity is much more of a Mystery religion than it is a theological one. At its core, it's really a great mystery, the mystery of the light and movement of the light, and energies of light. The Old Mysteries brought light in their way up to that time, and Christ came, and through the harrowing brought light into the underworld and changed that. It's more like before, one could say we had to search for God and now, through the harrowing, God comes to meet us. A much more active God. So that God comes to meet us, and we have to give up things and want to join into this process. But it's really that the significance came that now God came to humanity and rose in the soul for more access. And of course, he also illuminates the mystery of the resurrection. So not only is the spirit world penetrated more with light, but this is also true in the physical resurrection. This world, the light was brought into it more too, of course, so that we have more access in both worlds.

AV: I would like to return to that young woman that I had mentioned who is engaged in a journey through her own underworld. And you've mentioned the underworld and I'd like us to think about that a little bit because what's in the underworld exactly? What are we talking about when we refer to the underworld? You had mentioned before burdens and coming to understand the burdens that we bear, and with regard to the underworld it's also which we fear, what we desire, the underworld also includes the dead in the sense of the inheritance of the ancestral burdens that we bear, the underworld classically included Hades, a kind of spectral realm where the dead linger, and it didn't seem to be a very happy place, overall. So I wonder what you would have to say about the nature of the underworld itself?

RF: I think the first thing might be saying the underworld is another way of saying the afterworld. You know, throughout time there's always been a name given to it and the most common has been, this is our afterworld, the first world after death. There's a part of us that after we step over we encounter—

AV: After death, you mean.

RF: After death, yes. Stepping, crossing over to the other side. So here you have the realm of the dead, the afterworld, all the different names for it, but it is that world. And in that world, it has always been that then I have to undergo the confrontation with what I have become and all the things the soul has with it that have crossed over. But I think another point is that the soul always has that with it, I mean right now we're living in the spiritual world. The mystic has realized that we're living in the afterworld, we may not be aware of it, of course, because our lives are so closed off from what's really within us, but we carry the soul, every religion has al-

43

ways said that. Heaven and hell are with us and the underworld is with us, but nobody really thinks that through very much. All of those things, the demonic and the angelic, and who and what we are in the past, as we cross into the afterworld that is what we will have to encounter when we take that journey.

AV: What's the role of dreams in understanding the underworld and understanding our own transfiguration and transfiguration more broadly? What would you suggest to someone who's engaged in this journey and perhaps grappling with some kind of difficult circumstances and the kind of testing that happens on the quest? Because the astral and dreams are tied together, they're not totally separate categories, are they?

RF: No, not at all. And Jung of course, totally validates that. I think that there are hundreds of theories about dreams. I think basically what dreams attempt to do is to reflect to us, in sleep of course, the state and the *contrarium* of the soul. In other words, to bring forward what our monsters are. What our demons are. On the one side, presenting that to us so we can begin to do something about it. The other side is the light side, and that's all the great potential, and possibilities, and transfiguration of the soul and new being, what our own potential and signature potential might be. So I think it's a two-fold aspect that dreams will easily reflect. And most of the time it brings us our problem because that's what we need to deal with first or we need to pay more attention to. What our soul is still struggling with. Where is it strained? What wounds of the past have affected us, how are we running? All those things. I think we need to try to clarify that they are both of those. And with the idea of both we can learn about our problems and do something permanently. We can learn something about our potential so we could also do something about that. There's actually a book about dreams being the royal road to God.

AV: Certainly, some dreams seem really rich and symbolic and very much reveal something to us, or they reveal a whole cluster of things and other dreams seem almost more like flotsam and jetsam. Jetsam in the stream of consciousness, and not so significant. The significant ones are often charged in some mysterious way, I think Otto called it numen. Rudolph Otto referred to the numinosity not only in dreams, but also in different aspects of life. And it is true that there's a kind of hierarchy or a spectrum of dreams, and some could be referring to problems, but probably those fit more in the middle of the spectrum I think, that's been my experience. So there's flotsam and jetsam sort of dreams, then there're ones that are working out of or revealing or linked into something that one is struggling with, and then there are ones really so rich and so numinous that something else entirely seems to be happening with regard to that experience and there the dreams can actually be pointing toward or revealing what can happen, what has potential to happen, or what is in fact happening. So paying attention to dreams becomes a really vital part of this process that we're talking about. It's not that dreams are not simply the night's entertainment, they are a window into the soul and what's happening with the soul.

RF: Yes, yes. I couldn't agree more. And they are warning us to be on the journey, not just saying there is a journey but saying to be on the journey of the soul with both of its aspects, the dark and the light. And engage: I need clearing, I need deeper feeling, I need to actualize, I need to go somewhere. Those things are always being said in our dreams.

AV: There's something related to that which I wanted to bring into the conversation and that is the role of the arts and literature in what we're talking about. And I bring that in, literature— I'm using the word quite broadly, including here under the word "literature" all the great mystical works because although our conversation has been focused on the individual and individual experience, that actually has a cultural matrix. We live in a cultural matrix. If we're living a really full life our society, as a whole, doesn't really encourage that. And it doesn't support it in the way that it might have 100 years ago or 150 years ago. Which means that someone writing to me, saying this is what's happening to me, what do I do? That individual doesn't have really a rich tapestry of inner references, reference points. Someone who graduated university, someone even with a PhD, probably has not read Plato, has not read Plotinus, does not have—

RF: or Dostoevsky, or—

AV: Berdyaev, or—

RF: Berdyaev, yes. I think there's a new ignorance about literature. Almost a disdain for it. And yet, you say no to the greatest teachings of the soul as well as scripture that ever existed. These were all great explorers of the soul.

AV: It's such an interesting way to think about literature. Broadly understood, all literature is about the life of the soul, and the study of literature is engagement with the life of the soul. I can say, as someone with a PhD in literature and then secondarily in religion, including religious and philosophical literature, that virtually no one, from inside the university or outside the university for that matter, refers to poetry, fiction, the great epics as being about the life of the soul. But when you look at, for example, Beowulf, what is Beowulf really about? It's about a hero and a monster.

RF: Yes. The confrontation with the demonic element.

AV: The hero confronting the monster, Grendel. And it is, fundamentally, a soul journey. But we don't, that is the collective we, within the university, within education more broadly than the universities, don't engage with that and that is where things have gone so far awry. And coming back to and understanding the context in which the journey of the soul happens, that context is cultural and we have such an extraordinarily rich context and set of reference points yet, for the most part, those are devalued, ignored, dismissed, and not recognized. I think the most important part is that they're not recognized as what they really are. And that I think does a great disservice both to literature and art for that matter. And here by art I'm referring to the ancient religious statuary, the Celtic statuary, the paintings, the great inheritance as a whole, the artistic inheritance of all of Europe, and the European tradition. Both art and literature are about the life of the soul. And I think that this journey that you're talking about is impoverished without them. Our journey is impoverished if we're not aware of that and it's not our context.

RF: I think that's all very true. I would say I probably have learned more from literature about the soul than I have from most psychological writings. I think the death of literature in the modern world is one of the ways that people are sensing something is wrong. And I think what they're sensing is that in our society, these things are no longer being said through literature. Can you imagine in Russia, Dostoevsky being printed in the newspaper, and all these people following what he's writing and they can hardly wait for the next episode? Can you imagine that today, here?

AV: It's a very different cultural context that we have, you know I almost hesitate to use the word "culture," better to say "social" context I would say, in modernity with so much distraction. There are other avenues of expression that can also form context for someone who is engaged in this quest and engaged in this process but I think without the deep exposure to the broader cultural inheritance that we share, there's a great risk of impoverishment and also of an incapacity to fully participate in what we're talking about. Back to this example that I gave at the beginning, advice for someone in terms of what to read, where to go, where to turn for advice as one is engaged in this quest, entering into one's own underworld, and having to grapple with the difficulties and the traumas and burdens of not only oneself , but also others, and engaging this process as a transformative and transfigurative process. There are works that may be of help, and that's a place for us to begin to draw this conversation to a close because it seems to me that there are several things that we could think about going forward and talk about, including the roles that art and literature have and symbols in terms of the journey and undertaking the journey going on the quest we started with. That is one thing we could talk about but are there others that you can see, going forward?

RF: I certainly would like us to explore or refer to the importance of culture, of music, all the things that have always had the spirit. Religious literature, literature, all of which are in a kind of death right now. I mean we live in a world that people have no hesitation to take a Shakespeare and say, well, I'm going to completely ignore what he said and I'm going to modernize him, I'm going to inject my stupidity into Shakespeare so it's more relevant. I mean, I can't think of a greater act of ignorance, can you? I see this when I read so-and-so is clapping hands because someone brought Shakespeare up to date. Well, that's great stupidity.

AV: I think that certainly the themes of literature, music, theater, and art all come together as one thing we can talk about and another is male-female relationships, and how philosophy has important things to say about that and so I could see both of those, each of those having its own time to explore it for a little bit. As for now, I would say: what final observations do you have as we draw this conversation to a close?

RF: I think that the direction we're going in, the things that are coming forth from our explorations that are going to keep opening the path of the soul and the spirit and, I believe, in the end, help reveal the regeneration process of humanity, the rebirth in Eastern Christianity and the process of theosis. So I would just say that.

AV: The larger context is that a seeker is on a journey, and that journey includes a movement through the underworld, with reference to dreams, art, and literature. The process that you're referring to is ultimately, in a still larger context, theosis or deification, regeneration. That's the direction that the conversation as a whole is heading and perhaps that's the best place possible to end this one.

RF: That sounds good to me.

CHAPTER THREE

The Soul's Journey

Robert Faas (RF), Arthur Versluis (AV)

AV: The last time we talked about the Christ process, the soul's journey, the harrowing of the underworld, and our inner process. We'd also talked a little bit about the lack of support in society for that and for the inner life. I thought we might go back to the inner process, the soul's journey, the harrowing of hell and what that really means.

RF: I think that's a very good place to start because so much hinges on that. We need to ask, "What did Christ do in the underworld that was so different, so significant?" And I think to follow that is, what biblical references there are or scriptural references refer to Christ preaching, but if you really look into that—there is a book by Henry Corbin that makes the point it's really absurd to say Christ went down there and preached. He said what is often translated as "preaching" really has to do with showing forth. In other words, it's a proclamation of great depth, so in that, what he was saying and this makes sense is that Christ—and this is in some of the gospels, Christ appears—in other words—his resurrected being appears and that was the proclamation itself, it was just like a real person. If we meet somebody real, of course we can see that this is really real. Bringing his resurrected being of life into the realm of the dead was the proclamation, and bringing that being, which is to bring the energies of light and all of the reality of light to the departed, was the critical thing, because then one is bringing the sacrament, the mysteries of light, which are two mysteries of water and fire. And what we would say in Christianity are the baptism of light and the eucharist of light, and the revelation of light— that Christ brought those forward, so that the departed could now partake in those Mysteries, which were able then for them to undergo a cleansing and the growth to the nurturance of the light and light energies. They gradually reach a point of transfiguration so that they could enter the deeper world of light, which is often called Heaven or the deeper world of light transfigured—once reaching transfiguration, then the soul could go on.

AV: And that is a different perspective than what you could call conventional Christianity where there is a bifurcation—there is either hell or heaven. There isn't in conventional Protestantism, for instance, any space for what you're talking about for most people in terms of their beliefs. What you're describing is an intermediate space for growth after death, closer to purgatory in the Catholic tradition and that corresponds to what Jacob Böhme and Schelling wrote about in terms of the afterlife. For them, the journey after death is exactly that, a journey. And that's tied directly to what we do in this life, so even though it might sound to someone like what we're talking about is not part of the soul's journey in this life, that's actually not correct because what we do in this world is directly connected to what happens in the next and that's also very close to what Dr. John Pordage wrote about in his voluminous works that deal with afterdeath states or the posthumous range of possibilities.

RF: Yes. That's very true, and what has happened is that the Catholics and the Orthodox had this great battle about the nature of, for lack of a better word, purgatory, and there was some council and the Catholics more or less won the battle in the West, but what the Orthodox were saying—and this is exactly what Böhme says—they use the word "purifying fire"—that there is an intermediate realm that is basically a purifying fire. And the soul undergoes that journey, whereas the Catholics were saying, no it's more about punishment rather than transformation. And so there was a split—it's like each one of them had half of what a purifying fire is. The Catholics had the caustic part of it and the Orthodox, the healing part of it. And over time, because of those extremes, and then the Catholics making this into some sort of absurd doctrine, it really lost the existential reality of what that realm of purifying fire is in terms of the journey of the soul—what it really is like. As you said, each person is met individually by this fire and they have to undergo their own personal journey. It's neither a punishment nor just a forgiveness of everything, but really it's key to the existential reality of what a purifying process is according to each individual soul.

AV: And this—what you're talking about—corresponds to the amount of inner work and inner transformation that you go through in this life and what you work through corresponds to what happens on the other side. But there also is the possibility of not doing that work and so maybe what we could do is explore a little bit what that inner work is—what that transformative work in this life is and then talk about the absence of that on the other side as well. And one of the things I wanted to bring in is the dark night of the soul and the soul's journey toward the light, and part of that ties in with understanding the nature of evil and darkness. In Platonism, evil is considered to be the privation of good, and that's it. But Böhme and Schelling, and theosophy more generally offered a different perspective that the light and the dark are both part of the totality, and that for human freedom to exist, evil has to have some sort of relative—not absolute, but relative existential reality, and as we engage more deeply in the soul's journey, we begin to recognize not only love, but also wrath exists both inside and beyond us. Can we talk a little bit about the soul's journey in terms of this relationship between love and wrath?

RF: Yes, I think that it's so important to understand that the soul is more akin to the wrath side of God, in other words, the fire side; the soul is more like fire. Our spirit is more like light and that's more akin to the sun, which is the light. And so you have Father and Son and then when things fall or separate into warring wrath and love or fire and light, the soul comes into the world with this mixture. But there's that separation and they are at war with one another, so then for each individual what we do on our journey in life is either going to really promote that dark side becoming active and becoming very strong, or it's going to promote the side of light becoming strong, but I think Böhme would say—and Schelling too, that we have to deal with both the wrath and the light in the soul and that is only done ultimately through a direct facilitation of the Christ light coming into the soul enough times so that those two sides both have to undergo transformation and come over into the journey of the new being. What Böhme would say is that what's being formed on what we could call, our worldly astral-elemental level, there's an astral part that begins to be formed on our journey that reflects what we are becoming. Böhme has an interesting term, he called it the larvae—the mask of the soul, and ultimately that intermediate mask either grows in to a real sort of specter or it makes its progress in various ways into the light, but what the soul has grown into is what one then steps into the other world with, so whatever that has grown in the astral part of the soul, that's the intermediate part—that then is who we are, in other words, it is exactly what we carry all the time, it's what we have become existentially in the relationship between the wrath and the love.

AV: Right, because if we manifest in our lives, primarily the wrath, both generating anger and being angry, that then carries forward and that requires a lot of purifying.

RF: Yes, exactly.

AV: And that's why I was referring to Böhme's idea of love, but really, it's Pordage that describes this more specifically. He emphasizes the importance of love and loving, compassion, and kindness overcoming and transforming the wrath and Pordage describes that process in terms of mythology and planets—the planetary associations. It's not really necessary I don't think to go into the details of that process, which also Johann Georg Gichtel also wrote about.

RF: Maybe just except to briefly discuss the connection of the energies. The seven lamps of the soul or energy centers of the soul are like the seven planets and—so I think psychologically Böhme refers to the first four, the contracting, the expanding, the whirling anguish, and then the fire—and then on the other side, it's more of the light side and that would be light or love, sounding, understanding, and finally, embodiment of the kind of body one is. So just briefly, yes, it's what we become. We're becoming who and what we are all the time every day. It's kind of what we grow into, but that's literally the inner being within us. It's kind of a psychic being that's being created and at the end, whatever that has come into being, reflects who and what we have become and that's what then meets—has to meet the light and undergo the journey because ultimately that being has to be dissolved, so it's really like there's a second death on the other side in the process of purification.

AV: You're talking about physical death, but then the goal is to die to ourselves as part of the inner life in this life, and I think what you're saying is, if we don't complete that on this side, we can complete it on the other side.

RF: Yes. Yes, exactly, that the journey continues, and there have been some interesting studies on people who had terminal cancer and they studied their dreams over a period of time. A number of them died, of course, over time, but they saw within their dreams that as the soul approached the end, it basically made no difference to the soul that the body was going to die, because its work—it went on with its work up to the very last moment and then the sense was, of course, that it was just going to continue unabated stepping into the other world, but continuing the soul work that was necessary for it to do on the path of regeneration, which is quite comforting.

AV: It is, and at the same time, there is another side to this that I was alluding to earlier, which is what happens if one doesn't undertake work in this life. I also want to bring in the abandonment of the humanities in higher education today, and really across the entire educational system. The classics and the idea of literature and philosophy and theater for that matter, as reflecting the Mysteries and engaging with the mysteries of life, and with the Mysteries in a kind of general sense, that doesn't exist. But beyond that, there is actually a materialistic ideology that's developed in the academic world. It generates almost like a pseudo-religious fury or enmity and I suppose that can exist on the right, although I think conservatives in general tend to be pretty resistant to ideologies and being possessed by ideologies.

RF: Do you think it's because they [conservatives] still have a God?

AV: There's a religious dimension in the inner life.

RF: Yes, but with a lot of these people that you're talking about, there is no such thing.

AV: Right.

RF: Nothing exists beyond themselves.

AV: Right, so they become, to some extent, possessed by the ideology in place of religion—in place of I would say "inner life" is probably a better term because that's what we're talking about. People might misunderstand if we say just "religion." It's inner life I think that we're describing and there's a real hostility to that in the academic world. I have heard people say out loud "I hate the word 'spirituality.'" So why do you think there's this connection between Marxism, materialism, and this kind of ideological self-righteousness that's developed? What do you think is going on and what are the implications of that for people?

RF: I think in what you're saying there and what we've been talking about that they're delivering themselves to this darker element of fury or wrath that Böhme talks about. One of the principles of these true believers in all this cultic stuff is by and large, they're always really angry people and intolerant. And where's that come from? What's happening to these poor devils is they're delivering themselves over to the darker side of the soul and they are becoming more and more engaged with it and that's why I think you see so much rage because they really crossed into darker dimensions—that's basically the psychology of the dark side or wrath.

AV: That does correspond to what I've observed where there develops this hive thinking or hive mind and anger feeds upon anger, so you'll see a group of people become possessed by this self-righteous frenzy, and then in some sense, what that creates is also heresy and heretics. People that dissent are the heretics, and it's actually relatively close as a phenomenon to the Inquisition in Roman Catholicism during the medieval period where there's kind of a secular inquisitionalism that's developed.

RF: Yes, the dynamics of Communism in the twentieth century and all their trials and their purges enabled just that. If you didn't believe their radical ideology, you would go on trial and the intolerant would reign—it is absolutely appalling. The inquisition—it is that same dark psychology. If you feed these dark aspects of the soul, then it is what you are going to become.

AV: Right.

RF: And you could replace the ideologies with one another, but you still have what happens to the really ideological mind going on psychologically. In other words, they are psychically divorced from the light and love.

AV: Right and there are two aspects to it. Because they are often filled with wrath, hence you have this incredible death toll of Communism in the twentieth century, and what I'm seeing in the homogeneity of the left is that the same kind of dynamic is present. It has implications in terms of the afterlife because there are a couple of different things happening here. One is that Marxism and Communism are anti-spiritual and anti-religious overtly. Religion is the opiate of the masses and all that, as Marx said. So there are the anti-spiritual dimensions of Communism. But really it's based in a kind of rigid materialism, and so that corresponds to what we're talking about in terms of "I hate spirituality." Someone who accepts this kind of materialism, ends up in the afterlife, how? What's the consequence of this? That's the other dimension of this, because of course Communism left incredible death tolls—millions, tens and tens of millions of victims.

RF: Even more killed than the Nazis.

AV: Oh, by far. Far, far more. There's a book called *The Black Book of Communism,* and it's not a popular book necessarily, but it is a documented book and that is the trouble with the facts. They are facts, and there really is a vast death toll, and there is that part of it, but even ignoring all of that and just looking at a strictly materialistic—you could say hedonistic life, what are the effects of that on the afterlife? Obviously the effects of murdering countless people in the name of Communism or Marxism leads to an extremely negative afterlife because you have so much bad karma.

RF: To account for, yes.

AV: But even just ordinary materialism, what's the effect of that for the afterlife?

RF: I think we could say pretty safely in terms of what we're talking about that what they are doing in the inner world through the absolute denial of any kind of spirituality or spiritual existence, they are becoming just a hopeless materialist and the soul gets formed along those lines. Basically what the soul knows in terms of existence is really nothingness, and the soul becomes that nothing. In other words, it becomes what it has fed on, which is that there is nothing down to the very bottom. There's really nothing beyond the material existence. Then the soul has to inhabit what it has created in terms of its di-

64

rection and being, which is a horrible sort of dark nothingness.

AV: And that nothingness is really what we're talking about as our range of possibilities, which is for the afterlife, which is exactly what John Pordage wrote about.

RF: Yes, according to each person's giving over to it and feeding it, it would be akin to how deeply have they gone into it.

AV: So those who have generated all of this anger in themselves and self-righteous indignation and discontent—

RF: Yes, that in other words, they become inwardly monsters. Then you would have an idea of what they would become after death.

AV: And you would see that in the afterlife, so in some cases, it would be hell.

RF: In the afterlife there is a kind of psychic body to it and you would see it very clearly. There is absolutely no denying it there, so that a psychic body comes forward at the time of death for what one really is and it's palpable psycho-spiritually.

AV: And you've had some experience with that in terms of the court system because you worked as a court psychologist for some years, so you've seen in people aspects of this dark side among people who are incorrigible.

RF: Yes, and breaking that down into those who are either forced into kind of a therapeutic community or are dealing with it when they became more ready, but yes, but even more so, because in following what we're saying, I've also dealt with empty, angry, non-spiritual people in therapy and their dreams, were of course, terrifying, because at some point, they would dream about this. One I remember in particular, where this person was on the other side and there was nothing but this vast, darkness, totally alone, and then gradually, there far, far off in the distance, there was this small glimmer of light and the way that this person described this feeling of utter loneliness would be enough to raise the hair on anyone's head. But then the sense was okay, I understand, here's what I've come to, and we would talk about that, and that small, small glimmer of far-off light, I've got to begin to work towards that. I've got to begin to cultivate that light—in our terms, cultivate that light, better relationships, and just working the light more, and stop working this utter sort of empty darkness. I'm sure that makes sense how you could see that person, in the dream, had actually seen what they had become in that spiritual existential way.

AV: That would correspond with nightmares—that psychic life for some of these people that we're talking about have to be reflected in the dream world and the nightmarish dream world would correspond to what we're describing in terms of the inner life and then for people who are possessed by this wrath—kind of wrathful energy, or angry energy, and then people who are in this kind of gray nothingness of materialism, but see in the distance, a light. They see light and then those who have dreams in a dream life, that reflects the transformative path that those are really three broad categories, but they do describe—

RF: Yes.

AV:—different realities. Different, you could say, psycho-spiritual realities.

RF: Psycho-spiritual existential realities. Yes, exactly. And the soul is working to bring that out to the person and of course, the modern mind doesn't like the idea of dreams either, so it's sort of working quite hard, but not getting a lot of attention.

AV: You mean dreams are the way that the soul reveals what's happening?

RF: Yes, exactly. What true existential reality exists.

AV: Right.

RF: But in our dreams we see what we have become,. and what we're meant to become. So one side is working to the light, and the other side is working to the dark, which in dreams the soul is reflecting back to us. On the darker side of things, the shadow side of things, you see this is what you've become. And putting the two together in that way, kind of mirroring back to the soul its light or dark reality that it has grown into.

AV: Something that we've talked about before and that the psychologist Carl Jung did himself, was he would paint—he painted images of that inner life, especially during a very pivotal period in his life and—

RF: Yes, he undertook his soul's journey into the underworld and into these realms, into the dream realms and what we're talking about.

AV: In *The Red Book* for example—

RF: *The Red Book* is his journey in the spirit world and he called it the unconscious because that's more compatible with modern ideas. We can't talk about how the spirit world really exists, but it does, and that's what he was exploring.

AV: Right. And part of the path is to be aware of and recognize the importance of these dream images and dream experiences and to be able to become reflectively aware of them. One way to do that is by painting more, by drawing, sketching—

RF: Drawing, writing, exactly. Even pantomiming, some people can do it through dance, but something that exactly—that helps to bring it forward into the outer.

AV: Into consciousness so that—

RF: Into consciousness and into us—integrating into us. Not only into our awareness, but also into our whole being. Our journey, the soul's journey.

AV: Right.

[Break in conversation]

AV: We had discussed earlier the soul's dream life and the importance of reflective consciousness and drawings and writing and even doing paintings like Jung did or even dance—as soul expressions that—

RF: Imaging work, writing, body work.

AV: Different ways of integrating our psychic or our inner life into consciousness, and that was where we had left off. One of the things that I thought might be helpful for us to think about, since we've been using the term broadly and in a number of different ways—we refer to the soul and the soul doesn't refer to the ego as such, does it? What's the difference between the soul and the ego? We've been using this term and I wondered how you differentiate and why the soul is so important in the context of our broader discussion?

RF: I would say especially drawing both from Böhme and Schelling, my experience is that the ancient idea in the Scriptures is that we are a tripartite being of body, soul, and spirit, and soul is the basis of our individuality. Kind of the fiery individual principle—passion, things, self-determination, self-beingness and a fiery nature. The spirit is more of a light, and so oftentimes, even the modern artists, who may or may not believe in all these things, will consciously say, "Well my spirit moved me to make this drawing." So the old idea that there is a spirit and a soul and the body, and that on a psychospiritual level, that's also basically what we're saying when we use those words. That there's not only a soul, a psyche, but there's also a spirit. Those are a part of us.

AV: And the words "psyche" and "soul" in this context are, to some extent, interchangeable.

RF: Yes.

AV: But the difference is that spirit, being light, is beyond the soul, the psyche is—in the context you're talking about—intermediate between the body on the one hand and light, which is beyond, and light manifests you said as fire. And fire of course requires fuel, and fuel is in part the emotional and also in part, the realm of physical sensations, so those three are interconnected in a kind of dynamic way as I understand what you're saying.

RF: Yes. That's very true and I think one of the best is Böhme's work, but I also encourage people to engage with Schelling's work in *Clara* where he talks about the three-fold body, soul, and spirit, in the second or third part. He discusses this at some length and I think he pretty much follows what Böhme might say, but using his own language.

AV: So the reason that we've been talking about expressing one's dream life or inner life in terms of the psyche and soul is that that's the intermediate realm of transformation and that light works through the soul and we have volition, so we can also act and move on that volition. When it's directed toward the light, then it becomes transformative for the soul, and that's a process. It's a dynamic process. It's not simply a static relationship that we're talking about.

RF: That's very true and even to extend that, I know Böhme would say that the soul is directionality. If we go towards the light with the soul, then we enter into a transformative existence. If we go towards the dark, or a binding existence, or as he would say, the astral-elemental, and all three cross in fusion, then, he would say, you start losing your way, and you begin to produce the psychic creatures of the soul.

AV: Psychic creatures meaning, in some cases even demonic.

RF: Yes, yes.

AV:—but "creatures" is a way of expressing the wrong direction.

RF: Yes, creatures that are then produced. In other words, you would say that most people might think there's a choice between light and dark. That's true. Böhme would say that there were really three choices for the soul in a way that it was drawn by three elements primarily by the light, by the dark, the fire world, and by the astral-elemental world, and so he would say that humanity fell more into the attractions of the astral-elemental part of it. And so he would say that the time of this becoming entranced in world and losing our way and for some characters, there's a possibility of trafficking with and becoming a part of the demonic, which are of course extreme evil cases. Most don't give themselves over but are trying to struggle somewhat towards the light. So it's kind of a three-way warfare. It's a three-way drawing in a way.

AV: Let's talk a little more about the process of moving toward the light, because there are different aspects. There are different aspects to that because we've been talking about moving through a purgatorial journey dealing with the shadow, because of course a shadow requires light. A shadow is cast by something that blocks the light, and so perhaps by talking about that, we also are talking a little bit in the context of moving toward light.

RF: Well, yes, absolutely, and what could be said is that this is the whole nexus of it in a way. In other words, you enter into the realm of sacrifice and if there is no letting go, there is no sinking down into or towards the light of the mind of ordinary consciousness and stuff we hold on to and our shadow stuff. If we don't allow that to sink down into the light, no transformation can happen, so those are the things that we have to work on—in a sense giving up our attachments to it. The old idea of attachments is still very viable in this realm and if we're overly attached to things, then they form the creature inside of us. So I think the heart becomes—you're not going to do anything unless you can undergo some sacrifice and enduring through the life coming forward, and working on the dark things —the astral-psychic things.

AV: Working with the shadow and working with the kind of darkness that you're talking about is essentially also letting go. It's letting go of our attachments that in turn generate the darkness in the sense that we're the ones holding on and as we hold on, that in turn acts as a block, and so the shadow is essentially a kind of ignorance or ignoring or—ignoring the light and at the same time, holding on to whatever we think will buttress us, whatever "us" is in that context.

RF: Yes, exactly. It forms a false self and it grows. There is an accumulation—you go down this path and it keeps getting more. You become more entrenched and the creature, so to speak becomes stronger and larger and it only wants, in a sense, to have more energy and live. So it doesn't like the idea of having to sacrifice any part of itself—that's usually where the warfare of the soul comes in, the struggle of the soul. I mean as we all know practically, giving up stuff is not easy.

AV: No, particularly when it's perceived as our identity and by giving up—there are different ways to look at that, because giving up can be literal, like the desert fathers who literally gave up everything and went to the desert, but what we're talking about here is not necessarily that.

RF: We're talking about a more inner path and of course, if one is addicted to something in the world, I mean sure you have to give that up, you just can't keep feeding your addiction, but primarily what we're talking about is beginning to give up the old patterns and the shadow.

AV: And at the same time, being aware of the light and allowing that to manifest in us because the light is the transformative dimension here.

RF: Yes. Yes.

AV: And that's a way of providing a larger or a different context for some of the things we were talking about earlier. Because it allows people to see in a different way some of the same terms and the same things we were referring to earlier.

RF: Yes, and it's so important because we begin to really touch on the open secret of Christianity because what light are we talking about? What we're talking about is the light that embodies itself incarnated and left itself in this world and the other world so that it could be much more accessible so that the light can manifest. Christ embodies light and being light was really developed in Christianity, which of course has gotten somewhat lost, to say the least, a way of metamorphosis of transformation through light.

AV: And that's what we've been referring to and also pointing towards that there is this transfor-

mative path within the Western tradition—
Western European, but specifically the Christian
tradition, which is, for the most part, almost unknown. Böhme, the name Böhme, some scholars
are aware of it. They are aware to some extent—
occasionally you find reference to the Western
or Christian mystical tradition, but broadly
speaking, these are now, in our time, almost
completely occluded and so somebody who is
coming to all of this that we're talking about for
the first time, can be forgiven for being sur-
prised at what we're talking about because the
Christian mystical tradition is obscured even
within, and maybe especially within, many
churches. And many, many Christian denomi-
nations, and so there are many people who
think of themselves as Christian and yet have
never heard of, not only of Böhme but of Eckhart, or Tauler, or Ruysbroeck.

RF:—John of the Cross.

AV: John of the Cross or Marguerite of Porete.

RF: Yes, or William Law. Not a bit of that. I mean
I grew up Catholic, and Christian mystics—that
was the last thing I ever heard of. I didn't hear a
thing about that and—

AV: There's a story that I will mention again,
which is that I was attending my family church,
the one I grew up in, one summer day years ago.

RF: Is that Episcopal, Arthur?

AV: It was Reformed [Calvinist].

RF: Reformed.

AV: Reformed Calvinists, and there was an outreach minister who came in one Sunday morning, and gave a sermon in which he talked about Meister Eckhart, and that he himself had had a mystical experience, and he'd realized that was an important part of the Christian tradition, in fact the pivotal part. But after that sermon, he was not allowed to preach. He almost lost his job and he was not again allowed to address the congregation.

RF: I can so easily believe that because I think that's the great tragedy that happened to Christianity and especially in the West, there are these rigid theologies and hyper shame-ridden morality that has really crushed the whole Western mystical tradition.

AV: That's right and excluded it.

RF: Excluded it and then you have another relatively unknown tradition, you have the other side in Eastern Christianity, especially in the form of hesychasm, which has this long history of quiet and light and mystical experience, and nobody of course knew about that either, because Western Christians didn't know for a long time and many of them still don't—that there even is such a thing as Eastern Christianity.

AV: That's right, and it's not the case that everyone within the Eastern traditions are aware of their full tradition in the respects that we're talking about in terms of a transformative path in which the light is transformative and transmuting. And that is not necessarily known by everyone within that tradition either—even though it is more congenial to mysticism.

RF: No that's really true. Both of what you're saying there are quite true. I can count on one hand—I'm as you know practicing Eastern Christian and the number of the people that really know the Eastern Christian tradition of light and transformation of life through light, as I say, that would be the rare ones. And they just don't usually discuss that either in their upbringing, training, or in the ordinary life of the church, so it's like neither East nor West, even though the East has much deeper tradition, they don't really get these things and I personally think, or have to come to think, that's a huge reason that Christianity in the West has broken down so severely in Europe and even America, because the lack of that for so many years I think undermined the recognition that the soul could be helped on an ordinary level.

AV: I think that's right and there's another aspect to that, which is the disconnect with the older traditions that existed in Western Europe. You see that also in America to some extent, but especially in Western Europe, there is a disconnect from their own Pagan traditions and from the traditions connected to the land. One of the things that is important to understand in terms of the transformative tradition that we're talking about here is that, in for example, the work of Schelling, Schelling does not see those older traditions as something to be extirpated or as somehow the enemy, or that those earlier traditions of the Mystery should be cut off, but rather that they're reflective of—and prefigurative you could say, of this kind of inner transformation and there isn't actually an opposition here, but rather, a continuity between the ancient Mysteries and the Christian Mystery—including the Earth Mysteries, because what were the Earth Mysteries about? They were about the light, and the sun, and the sun cross. There are many sun crosses and those pre-date Christianity. And that's because those Pagan traditions also understood the light within the dark or within the cave where the mysteries took place, or the stone, they understood on some level that, and by rejecting that, somehow there's another kind of disconnect that also happened, both in Western Europe and in America, so people broadly speaking, are not aware that the Earth can be sacred or that there are sacred places in terms of the landscape and the reason that's important is you had mentioned earlier, body, soul, and spirit. And Christ—the importance of Christ's incarnation, that incarnation took place in a body in this world. There's been a disconnect from both the Earth, and from the body, and that's a consequence and a cause at the same time of some of the things that you're discussing in terms of our contemporary secular situation.

RF: Yes, very much so. The whole element of new being and resurrected being and a new heaven and a new earth is right there, in the Apocalypse and the scripture. Who picks up on those things? I mean Christ and the transfiguration of all things, which is supposed to be the ultimate end of Christianity. It doesn't say we just end up in a heaven somewhere—we end up in a new earth with bodies and as beings of light— the transfigured body as well.

AV: There are things in what you're referring to that I think would form the basis for a coming conversation, because we could talk in more detail about the light and the light-body. That's one theme. And another is the theme of relationship in terms of the transformative process, and transfiguration ultimately is what you're referring to, so a logical kind of process or progress might be to talk more about process next time and move toward a theme of light, body, and posthumous states and different posthumous states, which we've alluded to. And to this idea of transfiguration, which I think is vital and there's a lot that needs to be unpacked there or unveiled, so I can see some direction for coming conversations. We've covered a lot of ground, actually, because we've talked both about the process in terms of the soul, in dream life, and then about body, soul, and spirit. And now moving toward a kind of larger healing, which is what we were alluding to I think, both of us in different ways—the transfigurative healing that repairs the kinds of rifts and fractures that you were alluding to.

RF: Yes, transforms and cleanses and reunites.

AV: Exactly.

RF: Also picking up on regeneration, at the core here, there's a struggle between the idea of meditation and the idea of metamorphosis, which will take—that a meditative tradition, especially we could say in the Christian meditative tradition, may have the problem of leading to a nontransformative existence ultimately, as opposed to the way of light and transformation, which does lead to those things because for many people I think the West has had fifty, sixty, seventy years of a lot of people doing meditation—and I've seen a number of people in therapy over the years, who are not dealing with their shadows, even though they were very sophisticated meditators. But they weren't dealing with their anger and their brokenness from the past. They were going off into these mystical or quasi-mys-

81

tical states, but they weren't dealing with the soul struggles. And I think we could have an enormously fruitful discussion around that too — you know what I'm saying?

AV: I do know what you're saying and that's something that we alluded to in a conversation that we didn't include in this collection. I'm making notes for the next one, and I think you're absolutely right. It was part of an un-recorded conversation that we should really bring into this because I think we both have things to say about it.

RF: I do too, and I think it's critical right now for society in relation to what we're talking about, because we have so many people that are saying they're doing yoga, and they're doing this and they're doing that, and in reality there's no God, there's no light, and there's nothing more than maybe they're of course getting some good re-laxation out of that, but for so many that are "into this," that's a viable question. Is what they're doing ever leading them to any some sort of existential metamorphosis?

AV: Right. And that ties in with some other things that we could also discuss, which in-clude, as an example of what you're talking about, mindfulness. Mindfulness is a very posi-tive set of practices that people can pursue. But what doesn't it include?

RF: Yes, kind of an attentiveness, which in Western mystical tradition, is watchfulness. And go ahead, please.

AV: I'm going in the same direction that you are, I think, which is that it only goes so far because there isn't any larger context for it. And it's in fact deliberately secularized, as is much of yoga. And once that happens, it can be commodified, so you have Bikram yoga and all kinds of yogas, and they have their value. I'm not saying they don't, but they don't necessarily represent the kind of transfigurative path that we're discussing. There are some differentiations to make here, and I think we really probably should make those in the next conversation, because there is so much to discuss in this regard in terms of you could say separating the wheat from the chaff, and I think it's an important service to do that.

RF: I do too. In other words, I think we could say what really works for the soul and what ultimately doesn't.

AV: Right.

RF: I mean, where the hell does it ultimately take you?

AV: Right. I'm going to make some notes about this because there are a couple things that occurred to me. Maybe what we should do is draw this to a close for now, although now of course, we're on a roll. So, we don't want to.

RF: I trust we're going to get back into another roll.

AV: Yes, I think so too. And I think bearing in mind that we're bringing into the conversation people from a range of different perspectives. That is an important thing to recognize.

RF: I wholly agree with that, yes.

AV: And so the idea in all of this is not to offend or enrage someone who is a member of a church that happened to almost excommunicate a minister who mentioned mysticism, but rather to just say that something exists as an alternative to what you've heard about over and over. And that it's important to also be aware of that and to recognize what is possible.

RF: Yes. And that the great gifts of the light—in the sense become yours in this transformation of existence. I think that's another truly, of course key element, is that in the Christ light work, you don't have to have anything beyond yourself, establishing your own direction. You don't have to have status or whatever—it's just a matter of the directionality of the heart. In other words, I've always loved that the simplicity of this is for everyone and it doesn't make any difference what denomination you're a part of. So that's another trail we could go down.

AV: That's true, but that's also a good place to draw this particular conversation to a close— yet also what we're talking about is not a closing down, but an opening up.

RF: Yes. A continuing.

AV: A continuing—that's true too. Till next time then, Bob.

CHAPTER FOUR

Perennial Truth

Robert Faas (RF), Arthur Versluis (AV)

AV: Now that the technological issues are surmounted, when we left off, I thought it would be helpful to clarify some things by thinking about and drawing on the meaning of the perennial tradition. Often times, people think of today the perennial tradition or perennialism—or perennial philosophy, which is my own preferred term—and take this as meaning that all religions are the same. But that's not really the case and I don't think that's actually what perennialism is about. Perennialism is essentially saying that there is truth—that truth actually exists and that's an orienting point for thinking about how to understand different religious traditions in relation to each other, which is different than it's usually articulated. And I wonder what your thoughts are on perennial philosophy as a way of understanding different religious traditions in relation to each other.

RF: I think for me, it's very much connected to the eternal light. In other words, earlier, we were talking about the light, the magnificent manifestations of the light in all religions and because it's somewhat different forms, what happens with the perennial or the mystical philosophy is that it basically comes from a light and so it's an intellectual manifestation of the light, so it becomes put into thought, and so I think there is deep truth there as a guidebook to what are the eternal spiritual realities.

AV: And when you refer to light as a way of understanding it, the fact is that light here is a universal. Light is light. It's the foundation, the basis of life because without it, you wouldn't have life, and so there's a universal dimension to what we're talking about, as well as a particular dimension.

RF: Yes, very true. It is simply the unifying force. Light and inner light or spiritual light— you're talking about light in the physical world of that nature and that's what spiritual light within or on a spiritual level is, so you have this unifying force in a way that unifies all things and that's the light and then you have the reflection of that light, which is perennial philosophy.

AV: And that corresponds also to someone like Friedrich Schelling because Schelling was drawing on perennial philosophy as part of his perspective, but what he was doing was much deeper than what's usually considered perennial philosophy. And part of what Schelling was referring to has to do with transfiguration and the afterlife. One of the things that I wanted to develop here is an earlier part of our conversation, because we're thinking about or referring to the perennial philosophy and then we shift our focus to particular traditions—you are saying that there are really some distinctions to be made between some of the perspectives we've been talking about—the kind of transformative path that Asian religions have tended, in your view, to be somewhat different in terms of result and I thought maybe you could discuss that a little bit more.

RF: Yes, it kind of gets to the crux of what I'm saying. I think in the Asian traditions, you do have mystical and meditative process, but it doesn't seem to extend itself into the actual societies and everyday life of most everyday individuals in any profound way in terms of shaping their culture in ways in which the individual is sovereign over his own particular journey.

AV: That's not really accurate. You can see ample evidence, for example, in Japan—that Japanese Buddhism has had a transformative and vital effect on Japanese culture, which really couldn't be understood without it. Same with Tibetan Buddhism. They are transformative traditions. But with regard to the individual and

89

the individual path, I'll give you an example and maybe we can talk about the same topic from a different angle. One of the specialists on mysticism in the late twentieth century was Robert K. C. Forman, and he wrote about mysticism as "pure consciousness events," and he called that perennial psychology, but after he retired as a professor writing about mysticism, he revealed that his actual perspective was Transcendental Meditation. And as part of that, he wrote a book called *Enlightenment Ain't What It's Cracked Up to Be*, which implies that he's enlightened. Yet what he's calling enlightenment is definitely not the same thing as what that term would mean in Buddhism. In that book he's recounting how Transcendental Meditation has brought about this kind of "witness consciousness" as he calls it. It's a kind of doubled consciousness and I wondered if that's really what you're talking about when discussing the inner life and inner transformative life? Is it about developing the witness consciousness or a kind of enduring second consciousness or recognizing that?

RF: I think that it's about redeveloping a spiritual consciousness that has become lost in the fall. For a lack of a better term, before the fall, there was the heart consciousness that rose up and—what they usually call the mind was the recipient of that. A conscious mind was more like a receiver of things from the depth, rather than an independent entity in itself, so that ordinary consciousness has really, in a way, displaced and become like a little god and sees itself as supreme rather than recognizing that its job is to perceive and to provide from higher and deeper levels, and then help the being relate between the inner and outer worlds. And so the whole thing in a way means that—it even gets down to the whole idea of consciousness—the error has been to focus on consciousness rather than a change of being in itself, which is the result of transformative change, because that new being is the end for humanity—transfigure your being rather than just the concentration on consciousness.

AV: That's a really important point I think, but that is how he is defining mysticism and this is a quotation, I'm not just applying a label, because it's internal to what he's writing. He refers to a "pure consciousness event" [PCE] and to some extent we all, I think, or many of us at least in the modern world, emphasize that term "consciousness"—and consciousness as differentiated from the full awakening of being, and what you're saying is it's more than that. It's transformation of who we are at a level that includes consciousness, but it's not only consciousness. Is that what you're saying?

RF: Yes, exactly—that it's so much more than consciousness. That in the end, there is a supersensual being, in other words, from which our being has fallen. Our consciousness has fallen, and so it's ultimately a radical transformation of our whole being—the body, soul, spirit into its primordial higher supersensual state of being.

AV: Which is also love.

RF: Which is also love.

AV: And that's something that isn't really discussed very much. Much been written about mysticism and one label that can be applied to everything that we've been talking about in these conversations is mysticism. The contribution of this conversation, or one contribution, is to make clear that what we're talking about is more than rational or even super-rational knowledge. It's existential transformation of the whole being in the light of love.

RF: Yes, and that love is connected to the mystery of suffering. And that's the other thing: I think so many times these theories of consciousness have little to do with suffering and especially individual suffering. And of course, the part that love plays in all that. Those things are often not even spoken of, so it's like the suffering humanity and the mysteries of love are almost totally ignored, and so I think that's one of the great reasons you have society now plunging in any way that it can—to escape suffering. And you have the rise of addictions on just a tremendous scale. People used to be worried about repression. Well, you don't have much to do with repression anymore, but now you have addictions.

AV: There's another aspect to this, which I realized, and that is—to kind of give a further example of what you're talking about—there's a widespread tradition, and I think we can call it a tradition because it's become highly developed—of mindfulness teaching. It's in the universities. It's in corporations. Google has had mindfulness seminars. Apple has had mindfulness training—mindfulness is everywhere and I'm not saying it's a bad thing; I think it's actually a good thing in that developing people's ability to sustain attention—to be aware is a good thing. But what's missing from just being mindful or aware from your perspective?

RF: I think the same thing that we're talking about—is heart, soul, individual suffering, the reality of what has happened to one in one's past, all the things that go on in an ordinary human life are essentially not really a part of this situation. There is no replacing the existential questions—not really. And I think current mindfulness isn't much different from what we passed through in the 60s—that they used to go off the cliff about—the whole idea of higher consciousness. I mean, was it? Just the same old thing in a new bottle.

AV: And what you're referring to here, and what we're discussing, has depth. In other words, what we're talking about is not only height as in ascending out as it were, but understanding, and dealing with, and transforming, and working with what's in the depths, and that's what you referred to before as the burdens we carry and dealing with the burdens we carry as part of that.

RF: Yes. And that's very much what Schelling says in *Clara*. I think it's the physician [in the dialogue *Clara*] that said something about it's not from the upward/downward that we grow, but from the downward/upward—or in other words, from the depths to the heights. And I think so much modern thinking has completely cut out the heart, the depths, the deeper darknesses, and the deeper light, and all those are just not a part of it.

AV: Right.

RF: And so you can have this mindfulness and attempt at higher consciousness and whatever, but in the end, it's all like a charade because what does that have to do with your existential reality? And the fact that you're still facing death—what about the mysteries of that? And you're still facing all the pain and suffering of your existence and mysteries of love—what does it have to do with in regard to that?

AV: And with that in mind, I wondered if we could talk a little more—actually in my notes—

it's interesting that you mention Schelling's *Clara*. I've been reading that in the last couple of days and thinking about our conversation today, and I know it's a book that's important to you—but what do you think Schelling in *Clara* has to—

RF: And just to say when I sent you a copy of the different books that I've had translated, there should be in there a translation of *Clara*.

AV: Yes, of course. I've been reading that. What I'm really asking about is what *Clara* has to offer us because it's a book that we're going to bring out in a new translation, and it's a good thing too because the currently available one is actually almost unreadable. But in any case, the reason I'm mentioning it is I know *Clara* is important to you and it's been important in your life and I wondered what *Clara* has to say about what we're talking about here and about the death process in terms of our spiritual life.

RF: I think *Clara* is really grounded in the Christ mystery to the fullest extent. This is a book that talks about the mystery of life and death, the mystery of this world and the other world, which of course we're all intimately concerned with if we're not in flight from reality in some way or another. And so oftentimes it seems many people don't understand that *Clara* is really about conjoining the spirit world and the nature world. In other words, between this world and the other world. If you read the Christmas dialogue, it starts by talking about how the advent of Christ, the birth of Christ, was the reunifying force between the spirit world and the nature world—this world and the other world. And the character of Clara, who has lost her husband, is feeling joy about what that reality means to her and her ability to be able to not only see that as real, but also to be in communion with those on the other side who are the dearly departed. And so these are just monumental elements about the ultimate re-union between the world of the living and the world of the departed and the reunification of nature and the spirit world and the ultimate transfiguration of both.

AV: It's very rare as a book, because it includes a comprehensive vision of what you're talking about and I'd like to explore that a little bit more because I think there are things that are suggested by Schelling—since after all, it is a dialogue, not a treatise—so different characters are saying different things. It's very suggestive as a work, but one of the things that ties in with what we've been discussing is that it's a book essentially about how Schelling was working with sorrow—his own sorrow over the death of his spouse—and I wondered if we could talk a little bit about that, because again what we're discussing here is the depths and working with suffering, trauma, grief. What does *Clara* have to tell us about working with our own trauma and our own sorrows and grief and the burdens we carry?

RF: I think Schelling's theme—and this is really in the first part of the book on All Soul's Day—is resurrection. They've come to visit in this town and there's the ancient festival of All Soul's Day, and what he begins to say in that festival is that what helps us is the fact that Christ resurrected—that as a result of that resurrection, we are able to access that light to help us bear the sufferings that we need to bear and have to bear, but we don't do it alone. So essentially what he's saying is that the Christ-being is a living presence for us in our deepest sufferings—that the light is with us and that the light will help bear us through and transform us into this journey. The first part of the book is saying how we should really trust that there will be a resurrection and what that means is that the souls of the departed and the souls of the living will be rejoined and it will be like one family again. And the journey of Clara in the book, also reflecting in this, is her transformative state that she enters into—in the Christmas dialogue after she talks about the reunification of Christ bringing about the restoration of the spirit world with the nature world. She talks about the change she underwent herself—a sense of truly becoming flame. That's one of the deepest elements of Christian mysticism. I mean you have a history of both the East and the West. Western Christianity and people—Saint John of the Cross,

Böhme, always talking so much about becoming flame. And in the East, you have hesychastic masters who literally say to a disciple, "Why not become flame?" And so here you have Clara's soul and her journey literally becoming luminous flame and talking about how much this is helping her, so it's a journey, and it's really quite astounding.

AV: There is something I would mention too and that is the term—the name "Clara"—clear—meaning allowing light to pass through. Allowing the light. And so the name itself is conveying part of what you're describing.

RF: Yes and that's very, very true. And Schelling goes on, he talks about—like Böhme does—the purifying fire that many souls have to undergo in order for them to reach truly a state of clarification, a state of illumination after going through the refining process because only someone who has really become clear, can then have higher consciousness, but only after coming clarified.

AV: And that clarification—that is a result of a purifying fire and that purifying fire means transforming suffering by allowing the light to transform us and to resolve the suffering too. The suffering is something that we experience in our mind, and in our soul, in our body, and it isn't possible for those in themselves to resolve it. In other words, the mind on its own doesn't resolve the suffering without the transformative light.

RF: No, it's absolutely impossible for the mind to do that. And Böhme would say the mind by itself is simply bound to the wheel of anguish, so we just go on in the wheel of anguish with our suffering if there is no light.

AV: But *if* there's purification and *as* there's purification—then the process of illumination can happen. One of the things that's there in Schelling and I wanted to bring attention to this—is his discussion of the afterlife and there's a remark in there—and I don't recall which one of the characters it was that says this, but the remark is if we see in the physical world signs of the spiritual, why isn't it that we would also see in the spiritual aspects of the physical because they are complementary to one another? And so the afterlife is also a process and there is a whole range of possibilities there with regard to the afterlife, some of which we've talked about. But maybe we could talk a little more about that relation between what you were calling the nature world and the spirit world and how they are related to one another? I thought that quotation was really beautiful—that remark that just as nature is tinged with and shows signs of the spiritual realm, so too—why shouldn't it be also that way in the spiritual realm?—having aspects of what we understand as the natural?

RF: Yes, I think that's part of Schelling's genius, as well as Böhme's. There is a physical in the spirit world. It may be of a more subtle and finer material, but he says very definitely that we have two bodies. He said our physical body is obvious to us, but he said within the physical body is its spiritual body. Now it might be in a kind of a seed form because of the fall, but on the other side, that spiritual body takes on form that is just as powerful in terms of its reality as physical reality. So he says the whole personality, body, soul, and spirit—what we would say spirit body—are intact on the other side.

AV: And you're talking about also a light-body, which is not the same as the astral. People talk sometimes or write about astral projection and the astral—and the psyche. That is one aspect of the kind of ensemble that we are because there are different aspects to our being, but what you're referring to here, just to be clear, is the light-body, not the astral.

RF: That's right. In fact, what Schelling would say, and Böhme too, is the astral body that has become a reflection of our distorted being, has to undergo ultimately its own death in the transformative process. And out of that death emerges the psycho-spiritual light-body, and that then is able to go on to what they call heaven, but is actually a higher light world, because you now have the clarified light-body so that you can exist in a higher state, and the lower realms where these things have been happening here—you're able to rise out of that after the refining process.

AV: It's just a parenthetical note that there's also, in Tibetan Buddhism, a number of texts and traditions and different kinds of teachings about the light-body.

RF: A number of traditions recognize the light-body. And I think Böhme and others in Christianity identify it, but it's not really well understood. And in the light-body, and in Christianity, the resurrection body is also, of course, a light-body, but it's not the same thing as the other light-body, because it is a supersensual light-body in the resurrection as it was originally before the fall—that Adam and Eve in their highest state had.

AV: And you're referring to this final transfigured light-body, which was also described by Dr. John Pordage—and Pordage refers not only to the transfigured soul, but also to the range of posthumous realms that people might inhabit, so there's a whole spectrum of posthumous possibilities there. John Pordage writes about this at great length actually in these vast books that you've commissioned to have translated. He's writing about these different posthumous destinies and the different kinds of realities that souls inhabit after death and I wondered if you could talk a little bit about that because it's so germane to what we're discussing.

RF: Yes, this is found in scripture—and some of these authors like Pordage have recognized that Christ saying in my Father's realm there are many mansions, means that each individual person will inhabit his or her own realm and there may be a particular realm that he might be in for a while, but the number of individual states are almost infinite according to the number of individuals that are going through these processes. And so it has some subtlety to it, because it's all dependent upon what will happen with the light emerging and raising up and refining each particular soul—it will be almost inconceivably individual because each soul as we know is its own microcosm, its own world, and how it's lived and comported itself in all of life—that in turn helps shape and determine the course of transfiguration.

AV: But the soul in this process of transformation and purification is also inhabiting a world.

RF: Yes, an intermediate realm.

AV: Yes, exactly. That's referred to in some traditions of Sufism, discussed also by Henry Corbin in some of his books. Intermediate realm meaning it's a realm. It has manifestations that correspond to the state of consciousness that we're talking about—the state of the soul, the being of the soul.

RF: Yes. And Böhme and others—it's very intriguing, because the intermediate realm before the fall wasn't the kind of realm that it became after the fall. Before the fall it was like a medium of clear communion between the spirit world and the supersensual world. After the fall, that's when Böhme and others say because of the satanic fall, it became a different kind of realm—more corrupted—and it became more of an intermediate state or a place as long as the fall exists, but everything in that realm and all the souls in it are ultimately meant to complete refinement in transformation.

AV: And so ultimately the mystery of Christ is the complete penetration of all those different realms—that's something that we've been talking about before, which means ultimately the healing in transfiguration of all of those realms—however distorted they are—ultimately the healing power is greater.

RF: Yes.

AV: Otherwise, it would be a perverse sort of vision in which there couldn't be healing. Because it's kind of an either/or. Either the healing is transcendent and penetrates through all the realms or not, and it has to in order for there to be ultimate healing and ultimately liberation from suffering—freedom from the burdens of suffering, and sorrow, and pain.

RF: Yes, that's so true. And that in the end is like saying that Christ will not allow that, and that's truly the major reason that He came, which is to heal all the realms and all the beings back into and restore to an even higher level. If there are souls that absolutely refuse that, then my understanding is that they will be separated into the dark side, and it's in unity with the light, but there's a deep place where they won't become part of the light; they will stay a part of the dark. But everything else will be a part of the transfiguration of the light in the dark together.

AV: And I thought it'd be valuable to go back to the beginning, where we were talking about perennial philosophy and perennialism, because with regard to what we're talking about now, that term, although it's helpful as a kind of initial guide you could say, or a kind of pointing, it doesn't really capture the depth and the magnitude of what we're really talking about here. It's more like a reflection of it, but on a much more limited scale, so what we're really talking about here is much vaster than that.

RF: Yes. We can use it—a good kind of metaphor—it's like a beautiful flower that doesn't have—in that its roots are not into, let's say, the depths.

AV: You're talking about perennial philosophy?

RF: Yes.

AV: Yes, it's not that it's wrong. It's true. It's a reflection of what is in fact true in some sense, but it doesn't reach to questions of existential transfiguration.

RF: Yes. It's kind of like an abstraction rather than a full reality.

AV: And that would also then, you'd suggest be, to some extent, the case within what's sometimes called perennialism or Traditionalism as a particular movement—that too is not existential, but really highly or even incredibly intellectualized.

RF: Yes. Yes. I think the same thing can apply even though it is interested in dealing with the grail and questions of that nature, which are connected, but by and large, it seems to have become another kind of beautiful philosophic tradition, but without the roots of the suffering and the reality that we're talking about.

AV: I have to say I think this has been a really important part of our conversation because it so clearly helps to differentiate and create a clearer sense of what it is we're referring to and what's necessary.

RF: Yes and I think it really, really does illuminate that and I think it takes us into—and that may be where we'll go more next time—you have the perennial traditions, and then you have the Mystery traditions. I think the Mystery traditions are much more what you and I are talking about—the old Mysteries and the Christ Mysteries and all of that is of a different element and I think that's what we'll probably be looking more deeply in the way that Schelling was doing.

AV: Right and that's what we started—our conversations are to some extent spirals.

RF: Yes, yes.

AV: We started at the very beginning, addressing somebody who really had no idea that there was a deep path within the West, within Christianity, in the way we're talking about and we went through different aspects of these—of the path itself in early phases and how you deal with different aspects. We talked about the shadow and working with the burdens that we bear, paying attention to our dreams, working with dreams, and now we're moving to talking about how what we're discussing is to be understood in relation to some of these other terms and ideas and traditions and what distinguishes what we're talking about.

RF: Yes.

AV: And now it's a question of moving forward into the next chapter and I'd like to draw this conversation to a close. We're just about at an hour. I wanted to summarize it a little bit—summarize where we're at. Is there anything you wanted to add to that or to clarify?

RF: I think just that we are beginning to move into what you might call the Mysteries of the Risen Christ, that the church and conventional belief systems have not done that very well. We have lost a lot of that, but it's clear that the Mysteries of the Risen Christ really connect with the Mysteries of the ancient world. What would your summary be, Arthur? Or do you want to respond to that?

AV: I do, because we've alluded to that before, but what you are drawing attention to is what ties together all these different aspects of today's conversation. Because we're talking about the afterlife, and different aspects of the afterlife, and transfiguration, and what within this tradition is the means, where the transformative power is, and that is the light of Christ, and the Christ Mysteries. So it's only natural that having alluded to different aspects of the afterlife, in relation to this life, it's only natural that in the next conversation we talk more specifically about what we can roughly call the Mysteries.

RF: Yes, yes. That sounds really good and I think we can illuminate that, because we've both experienced that what's happened in the modern world unfortunately is that the Mysteries have collapsed and you have an intellectualized world, but you don't have the Mysteries anymore. The Mysteries were what made possible for the individual his changes, his transfigurations. That really only happened in the Mystery context.

AV: I can see the direction we need to go and you're absolutely right and I want to at least allude here also to some of the great visionary poets as part of this—Dante and also Petar Njegos.

RF: And I believe they were Mystery writers.

AV: Oh, absolutely. No question.

RF: I think that's what they were really doing even though they might've had theological dimensions, but really, they were tracking the Mysteries.

AV: And so we'll draw this conversation to a close and we have our way cleared to the next one.

RF: All right; that sounds really good.

AV: Perfect.

CHAPTER FIVE

The Path is Open

Robert Faas (RF), Arthur Versluis (AV)

AV: Earlier we were talking about the transcendence of subject and object— the transcendence that's represented in Böhme's work by the Ungrund—and there's a German writer, a contemporary by the name of Willigis Jäger. I'm sure you're familiar with him. He's in your library I have no doubt, and he ties together the different traditions of mysticism, but he represents primarily the mysticism of Meister Eckhart. The transcendence that Jäger is referring to—and he's both Catholic monastic and simultaneously has full training in Zen Buddhism—focuses on or draws on the tradition of Eckhart and Eckhartian transcendence in a very pure way. I wondered what you had to say about that tradition in relation to what we've been talking about, which is the path—the inner life and the inner journey.

RF: Could we stop for a moment? There's a book that I want to refer you to about this and I know right where it's at, Arthur.

AV: Just go get it and we'll resume in a moment.

RF: Okay.

RF: There's a book by Thomas Matus [*Yoga and the Jesus Prayer*] that really explores the Eastern and Western dynamics of yoga, prayer, meditation, especially in relation to Eastern meditation practice. It's quite well done. And it really brings up the differences as well as similarities, which is, I think, what your question refers to. With the Eastern, it's going into the inner world and becoming illuminated; it focuses more on transcendence. And the West—I think the Christ direction is really much more of a transmutation of one's being and the world. You have to go within of course to begin that journey, but more and more, the light is meant to come into one-self, transform oneself, including one's body, as well as the world. And so I think there's a difference about the light coming into the world ultimately in the West in Christianity and ending up with a transfigured being and transfigured world.

AV: It depends. You're referring to yoga and that particular book looks at Hindu yoga traditions with regard to the Jesus prayer and the Hesychastic tradition. What I was referring to was really the importance, the significance of what we could call sheer transcendence, which is so important, so central to Eckhart. I actually have a small collection that was published some years ago of Eckhart and in it Eckhart says things like, "To know God is to know him as unknowable. As the master puts it, if I must speak of God, then I will say that God is in no way reachable or graspable and that I know nothing else about him. Whatever Dionysius Areopagite conceives, God far transcends it. There is no knowing him by likeness. In unknowing knowing, we know God, in forgetfulness of ourselves and all things, up to the naked essence of the Godhead. Dionysus extorted one of his disciple's friend. Cease from all activity and empty yourself of self that you may commune with the sovereign God." So those are just a couple examples of Eckhart's sermons concerning sheer transcendence and what I was pointing toward and wanting us to look at is not so much the theme of East and West as such, but the theme of the Ungrund and Nichts—the sheer transcendence that is part of what Böhme refers to. Ungrund is different than Nichts. Nichts is literally nothing—no thing prior to all things and that plays a role in Böhme's cosmology, but it's also part of the metaphysics of the Böhmean tradition and it's there in Orthodoxy. It's there in the whole range

of the Orthodox transition and Hesychasm because it's focused on the question of transcendence—the nature of transcendence is the central aspect of the Dionysian tradition that at the
beginning of Christianity and that manifests itself both in Western mystics—Western European mysticism and mystics like Eckhart and
then later Böhme—and also in Orthodoxy. And
because this is so central, this theme of sheer
transcendence, which is repeated many times in
Eckhart's work. I wanted to start with that because our conversation so far has focused on the
path—the inner path of the light, but we haven't
dealt with or discussed different aspects of this
element of sheer transcendence—transcendence
of subject and object, which is so central to all of
mysticism. I wondered for that reason what you
had to say about this—maybe starting with the
themes of Ungrund and Nichts in Böhme.

RF: Yes. I think starting with the Ungrund—
there is all of this mystery of course of not only
transcendence, but manifestation as opposed to
non-manifestation. If we take the Ungrund and
the state of let's say un-manifestation—God is
unmanifested being-ness, which is unknowable.
And then in Böhme the first movement towards
manifestation is the will as the dark will—the
Father, the fire, towards manifestation, which is
the great mystery, and Böhme remarks that this
is what we can't know—why it is that God from
the Ungrund decided to manifest his own be-

ing? That's too great of a mystery. And then in becoming Fire, immediately the Light rose as well, and that was the first dying, he said—the first sacrifice. The fiery will had to give over to the rising of the Light and then according to Böhme, then there was God's full manifestation and then we can't forget Sophia, who is the light-body of God. What's the mystery of the body of God? The light-body of God, meaning the mirror of God, whereby God can see his own being. So I think the idea of transcendence is directly linked with the idea of manifestation. It's central, and Oetinger said that all of God's ways tend towards manifestation or embodiment, so maybe the question is: what's the relationship of transcendence to manifestation or embodiment?

AV: That's a really interesting way to look at or introduce this because essentially in Böhme, the Nichts, the nothing, is prior to all manifestation. It's —

RF: Yes, the un-manifest.

AV: It's the un-manifest out of which manifestation emerges—it's the ground, you could say, the ground or the fundamental, which Nicholas Berdyaev calls meontic pre-being or transcendence of being, out of which being manifests. So a flipside of this, and this is referred to in some of the images of Dionysius Andreas Freher: another way to look at manifestation is that the Nichts surrounds it. In other words, manifesta-

115

tion happens inside this matrix. In one illustra-
tion in particular that I'm thinking of, the illus-
tration has the word Nichts on the outside and
manifestation is taking place in the center on the
inside as it were in this diagram or image, which
is a reversal of the way we normally think of it,
but basically it's that the Nichts or this transcendence pervades materiality, in other words, it
pervades manifestation. It's there all the time as
the not-ground or the base because Nichts is
conceived of or understood as Ungrund in
terms of manifestation. It's the not-ground of
the ground. Does that make sense?

RF: Yes, like you, I've often been really im-
pressed by Freher's drawings, especially the
thirteen figures as you know. Those thirteen figures really talk about this mystery that you just
referred to, and how first there is the un-manifest, and then comes the will towards manifestation. And then the rising up of the light and so
the un-manifest is all—and as it becomes manifested, all of that and with the light-body, all of
that is utterly transcended. That's God's being
before the creation of the universe.

AV: I think what you're saying is that manifestation is a reflection of that transcendence, so
manifestation exists as a mirror—the mirror of
Sophia as you were mentioning, which is a reflection. It's reflective. In other words, it's transcendence becoming aware of itself through
manifestation.

RF: Yes. And then as Böhme would say, —the only way maybe to talk about it is that then God can see his own images, which are not yet—they have to go further in creation to manifest with more bodiliness so that they become more tangible. So there are different degrees of tangibility, of embodiment even before the fall. That's the mystery of the transcendent becoming in a way, embodied, at different levels.

AV: So when we're talking about the mysteries of the Nichts and Ungrund and transcendence of the self-other division, that is, the sense, the illusion that we're completely separate autonomous beings, the mystery of transcendence is indivisible from the mystery of manifestation because manifestation is actually about coming to realize that in different ways. In other words, the whole process that we're talking about and Böhme is always referring to a process in his writing, that process—if we want to encapsulate it in a term or in a phrase—that process would be divine light manifesting and the divine images manifesting in order to realize their own intrinsic nature.

RF: Yes. And that nature was a pure manifestation before the fall. In other words, as Böhme observes, in the fall what happened was the loss of the primordial light-body—the pure body that reflected the transcendent within, and as Böhme described, it was like a burning candle that you introduce foreign dark matter into, and the candle's light gradually goes out. There was a withdrawal of the light-bodiness in the manifestation. And then there is the withered body, so to speak, that in a sense we began with after the fall.

AV: And the fall is what you're referring to as the way of understanding the existence of suffering and evil in the world as a—

RF: Brokenness, yes.

AV: The brokenness in the world. And the inner path that we're talking about is really a healing—it's about the healing of that brokenness or the healing of that fall. The word "fall"—really what we're referring to, and it's there in Böhme, can be understood as mythological. It's conveying a truth in symbolic form and that symbolic form is the myth of the fall, but it's the fall realized as suffering and the existence of evil in the world and part of that also is the restoration, the return, and the return is return of the light through practice, through contemplative life—manifestation of the light within manifestation.

RF: Yes, yes. And that's exactly what Böhme would say on two levels—first it happens spiritually. The light, which is also, as Böhme writes, the same thing in many ways as the body and blood of Christ in a high sense—that Christ's body ultimately is the same body that Adam had before the fall, which is the pure body of light. That's Christ's light-body. But Böhme would say in the inner world, in death, and as a result of purification, that the inner body of light was first—their inner spiritual body of light and the outer one—the paradisal one. And that the inner one first is reconstructed again after the purification and that's the body that one is able to finally enjoy the inner heaven or luminous world there until the time of the resurrection. Böhme would say that the final physical body of light does not come until Christ's return.

AV: By physical, you're not referring to matter in the sense that we would understand it in materialistic science. You're talking about matter in a metaphysical context—"physical" in a different sense.

RF: Right, because there are two forms of matter. There's the matter that we know now, the fallen matter, so all we know what fallen materiality is like. But within that is the light matter and the resurrection reasserts itself by burning away fallen matter until that matter becomes light materiality again as it was before the fall, and that portion that Adam was in in the world before the fall—the paradisal portion.

AV: And Nicholas Berdyaev in his books—I have a couple of them right here. One you had mentioned, the introduction to *Six Theosophic*

Points. He refers to the importance of this restoration that you're talking about, this illumination in terms of freedom. And he actually even invented a word, which is "meontic," referring to the transcendence of being. And the light-body, the kind of physics of light that you're referring to, has to do with restoration and illumination, but it could also be understood from a different perspective, Berdyaev said, in terms of freedom and that freedom is meontic. He introduces the kind of privative implication—the *me* is what comes in the word *meta* as well. Meontic, the transcendence of being, and that's really what we're referring to. The fallen world is suffering and brokenness, but the meontic, using Berdyaev's term, is a source of freedom. I think it was a real insight, shaped by the fact that he had to see the onset of communism and the massive suffering it generated. He saw that clearly, but he also saw a path to freedom, so that's one of the reasons I wanted to bring in the themes of Ungrund and Nichts. But I wonder what you would have to say about Berdyaev in relation to what we're talking about now—freedom and the physics of light?

RF: I think there's so much truth in that and either through his own great spiritual insights or through his reading of Böhme and Schelling, he saw freedom as absolutely central because in Böhme—let's just say God the Father had to perform the first act of freedom. He could not stay in his dark fiery will and just let that manifest itself. That was the first act of sacrifice—the first dying—God did that to his own being, so that the light could rise. Now this happened instantaneously with God, but that sacrifice refers to just the freedom in God. There's the whole prototype that everything then is based on, and Böhme's metaphysics of the soul—it's the soul is drawn to directionality at all times (toward the light, the dark, or the astral-elemental)—the *contrarium* of all things. Only God made that irrevocable free decision to let go of that will to the Light and then the Light overcame, and became union. And I think Berdyaev is talking about freedom being grounded in God's own being.

AV: Freedom is grounded for Berdyaev in the meontic, meaning the transcendence of being [*ontic*]. So what we're talking about is beyond the realm of being in terms of separated subjects in a world of objects. What we're talking about is truly metaphysical, and I think that's why Dionysus the Areopagite expressed things in the way that he did when he wrote that treatise *Mystical Theology*, which describes the transcendence of being, the transcendence of subject and object, as a series of negations, which became known as the negative way [*via negativa*]. And understanding light, not only as physical—it manifests also in physical light, but what we're talking about is not physical light strictly speaking in the way we would measure at 186,000 miles per hour. We're talking about something else, which is metaphysical, and Dionysius expressed it this way. He said, "I pray we come to this darkness above light. It seems to me we should praise denials differently than we do assertions because we climb from the last things up to the most primary and as we do so, we deny all things so that we may know that unknowing, which is hidden from all those possessed of knowing among beings." So what he's referring to, he says, is not a material body; it has no shape or quality, quantity, or weight, it's not perceived or perceptible. There is no change, no decay, no division, no loss, no ebb and flow. It's not soul or mind. It's not imagination. It's not speech. It can't be grasped by the understanding since it's not knowledge. It's not even truth. There is no speaking of it. There is no name. There is no knowledge of it. It's beyond assertion or denial. And then he concludes by saying, "It's got a preeminently simple and absolute nature free of every limitation, beyond every limitation, it's beyond every denial." And that sheer sweeping away of conceptual structures is what Berdyaev is drawing on when he refers to meontic. It's absolute transcendence and within that, the light manifests. But it's not light the way we ordinarily think of it.

RF: No, we could call it the supersensual light. But yes, there's spiritual light, astral light, and physical light.

AV: Three different kinds of light.

RF: Three different kinds of light. And these lights—the spiritual light is deep within the fallen world, the world of phenomena and all that, but it is not detectable by any worldly means—only soul or spiritual means. It's not detectable by any physical instrument or faculty as we know it, nor is it readable, no matter how sophisticated your instruments. It is beyond the world. And Böhme was pointing out that's what the world lost. It lost that light that penetrated through it and then withdrew in the fall more into itself and then Christ came to bring—Christ the Light came to bring that back—all back into manifesting itself in the materiality.

AV: And the practice that we've been alluding to during these conversations is a practice of manifesting that light in the world and that's essential to the theosophic tradition.

RF: Yes, because through purification, we allow more light to come through. It always has to be through the process of purifying those fallen aspects of the soul or body so that light can manifest itself. It can't ever manifest itself until those processes or metamorphoses happen, but it's building a new body all the time through that metamorphosis internally and ultimately externally.

AV: Externally in the sense of us as humans who are conscious and conscious of—and manifesting the light. Acting as means of restoration of that original light that was there at the very beginning; it's always present. But at the same time, it needs to be manifested through the practice that we've been alluding to.

RF: Yes. Schelling has a wonderful word. He would see us as the mediators between the world and the Divine— that God aids us and we were meant to be the mediators of raising up— bringing light into the world and that if we had stood through in the fall, that we would have been solidified in that. But in that great struggle of the fall, we went too far over to becoming entranced with that part of the universe that's material and warring as a result of the initial fall of the angels. That trial was a standing-through, so now we stand through the trial again—and we become the mediator of bringing the light into the world as best we can through the processes of mediation. So we are God's co-creators or helpers in raising up and bringing the light into existence.

AV: That's what the Benedictine monastic Willigis Jäger was referring to. He was referring to the fundamental need that we have for wholeness and he actually—in German, capitalizes that. The word isn't of course wholeness, but in the English translation, it's conveyed that way, and wholeness is his way of referring to this healing and the healing takes place through this restoration—the way Jäger puts it when he says—and this is a quote—"When one emerges into creation, it becomes polar. Unity crumbles into multiplicity." And from a human perspective, we perceive things in a way that brings us suffering, but in some sense, we're deceived by the way we see things. We see things in a polarized world, but actually that's not really correct. What we're seeing isn't ultimately real in the sense that it's perceived through this brokenness that you're referring to, through the suffering that comes from this state of dividedness, and the practice of illumination is also the practice of wholeness of healing, which is healing of that dividedness.

RF: Yes. I might add that things have to be recast and ultimately it's just not a matter of perception, it's a matter of—yes in their true form they are not divided, but they have become divided in the fall and they need to be recast and in a sense, melted down, and then brought back into that harmony of their opposites or—and that process of illumination—it's always preceded by the death and end before illumination. There is always the tough business of purifying.

AV: And that tough business as you refer to it is expressed symbolically in alchemy and the alchemical —

RF: —the alchemical work, the torture of the metals—the torture of alchemy.

AV: Right. Alchemy provides this language and imagery for understanding how this happens, how this works. Can you say a little bit about alchemy in relation to this path that you're referring to?

RF: Essentially we could call the whole path an alchemical path. It is alchemical in that it is about purification, the transformation, the bringing out of the new body, the Christic path, all of this is purely alchemical. I think alchemy is the best reflection of the Christ path that there is.

AV: And what are the main stages if we're going to give someone a kind of shorthand map of those alchemical stages, what would that map have on it? What would be the base colors and the intermediary color and the upper color? What would that look like?

RF: I think that the three basic ones would be the nigredo or blackening, and then the whitening and then the reddening. And of course, the blackening is the raw purification stage. And the whitening is when things have become cleansed—then we're in a higher state but there still is more to be raised up. And then that—continues to be whitened. And then that ultimately ends in a final stage—the reddening.

AV: And by reddening, what would you mean? What are you referring to in terms of the red?

RF: The red is associated with gold—red and gold. It's like the final stage of transformation. John Pordage talks about those who have gone through the first two stages and in his treatise he wrote to a woman practitioner, or a *soror mystica*. In that treatise, he says you've come so far and you've come to know what it is to purify and bring things to a state of purification, but he said there's still a work that's left. There's another and a deeper work, and that's the reddening where you have to purify that which has been purified on a deeper level. So it's like in the Bible where it says you've swapped out seven devils and then if you're not careful and keep working, then seven more will come in worse than the ones before, and I think that's referring to the need for continuing work.

AV: So you were referring to the seven devils leave and seven more come in, which means that purification is a process—it's not something that happens just once and then that's it. That there is a process of purification and —

RF:—and a secondary one, yes.

AV: And a secondary one, so it can be understood as a process—more like a spiral in the sense that you return to the same place, but you're in a different relation to that place, but there is still purification to be done, so we're revisiting the same from a new vantage point, but at the same time, still undergoing purification in order in a sense, to go still further.

RF: Yes.

AV: And with regard to the reddening, you mentioned red/gold, and of course alchemical language draws on gold, but the other part of that is the red, which is the red of the heart and I wondered what you would say about the role of the heart and one could also say the heart and blood, but we'll say the heart in this process?

RF: The heart is the alchemical workshop where this is fundamentally taking place and then spreading out, so to speak.

AV: And as it spreads out, as it manifests, there is a German word that is used in the translation of Pordage, *barmherzigkeit*

RF: Warmheartedness. *Barmherzigkeit*

AV: That *barmherzigkeit* which could be understood as literally the warming or as the transformation of the heart, but it also is referring to mercy and compassion and kindness and love, so there is a role that love plays in this transformation that happens in the heart's workshop.

RF: Yes, and in fact, that is essentially the word that Böhme uses to refer to the being of Christ again and again. He says Christ is *barmherzig*, the warm-hearted one and that his fire—Christ fire, the light fire, the love fire, as Böhme calls it, this love fire is exactly what we are talking about. It gradually melts things and there's a continual warming that goes on within one-self—from the fire of the Warm-hearted One.

AV: And that enlivens it. It's at the heart of this process that we're talking about because it's actually the divine warmheartedness, or the divine love, the divine compassion, manifesting itself in manifestation and that's part of this light process, so the light in this metaphysical sense we're referring to—not in astral or physical only—but really metaphysical light is indistinguishable from or indivisible from this quality of warmheartedness or love.

RF: Yes and I would even say that tells us the real truth of why Christ manifested—Christ had to embody his warm-hearted light-being into this world to give it the process so that it could be able to do that. Christ didn't come as a teacher, essentially, he came as what we might call the supreme alchemist that had to bring all the warmheartedness back into and re-melt the world and all that He did and went through and the resurrection, the harrowing, all those things—those are supreme alchemical acts by the Warm-hearted One. In other words, he didn't come to teach, he came to overcome.

AV: And that melting is a melting of also our own rigidities.

RF: Absolutely.

AV: The structures that we inhabit and that we've enacted or enabled—these kinds of rigidities that are blocking all of that. What you're suggesting is what's part of this process of melting. Because we're not talking about light in a sterile sense of physical light alone, we're talking about light in terms of a process, and that process is directly linked to the manifestation of this warmheartedness and melting light and love and what it's melting is our own structures and limitations and rigidities and brokenness.

RF: Yes, exactly. Our rigidified contracted self—all of its history of grasping and the woundedness and waywardness—its whole history that has become psychically embodied within us and this—and Böhme would call it again this creature—those are our creatures that we've raised up over time. Some inherited from our parents and the past. Some that we have of course fed, in our own ways of being. And those become structures, habitual structures.

AV: And so this alchemical process is ultimately transmutation of the self, meaning revelation of a deeper understanding of who we really are, which is actually beyond the self that we think we know because what we identify with are all of those things that you're referring to. Böhme refers to them as creatures, but they can be understood as manifesting in terms of urges or fears. But what you're referring to is beyond that, and the process is challenging.

RF: Yes, it is, which is why in alchemy we are talking about torturing the metals—it's torturing. It's hard work in the process. It's not an easy process to have one's shit melted away.

AV: And here what we're talking about, especially the nigredo [the blackening], this—again, this is a cycle. We're not saying there's a nigredo phase and then that's it. You're done with the nigredo, you don't need to deal with it anymore. It's just —

RF: It keeps cycling, right, between darkness and shadow and shadow and darkness, but like you said, it's a spiral.

AV: So one is dealing with the nigredo in different context over time and there's a slow process of illumination.

RF: Yes.

AV: Which can be understood as the whitening.

RF: The whitening, the illuminating, yes.

AV: The white, the illumination. Yes, the albedo,

as opposed to the nigredo. But then within that is also the rubedo, the red.

RF: The final transforming, yes. I think one of the best indications of alchemy is the *Rosarium Philosophorum*, where you see a couple going through the first process, and then they come to integration. But then there's another process, which is the reddening, and then they come to an even more fixed integration and then in that last one, there is a figure of Christ in the final image—resurrected Christ.

AV: Right, so in the *Rosarium Philosophorum* you actually see the process we're talking about manifested in different images and the final image is that of the Risen Christ.

RF: Yes.

AV: And of all this process can be understood, and this is directly from Böhme reflected again in Berdyaev, and present already in Dionysius way back in the very beginning of the Christian era in the period of late antiquity, this whole process is taking place within and manifesting within this sheer transcendence, but one has to go through the process in order to move toward wholeness and toward understanding within that. It's not that this absolute transcendence that Dionysius was referring to exists, and that's all one needs. It's that it exists, but there's a process to undergo and to experience and to purify oneself and others and move in the direction of greater and greater illumination. This process takes place within the Nichts, in other words the Nichts surrounds everything in some sense, but the process is necessary.

RF: Yes, absolutely necessary. And Böhme even refers to it, interestingly enough, which is—I think he is a great alchemist in his own way of course—he said it's the Christ process. That's what he calls it and so few commentators on Böhme have really spent time saying well what does he mean here? or going into—they describe his cosmology but they don't really follow his way, his Christic way that he's talking about almost all the time—almost everything that he's writing is about this process.

AV: And that's the importance of Böhme within this larger mystical tradition that we're alluding to here, because Böhme represents a synthesis of alchemical tradition with this tradition of Eckhart that goes back to Dionysus; it's all there. Everything is there within Böhme and it's actually not in conflict with Orthodoxy. We can understand all of these together in a larger kind of global perspective as different aspects of and illuminating the same process.

RF: Yes, I think that's absolutely true. I think in both Eastern and Western Christianity, they might call it by different names, but whether we call it *theosis* or divinization in the East, or the process of regeneration and rebirth in the West, we're talking about exactly the same thing. And they go back to the very beginning of Christianity in having this process. Think about Dionysius the Areopagite's three stages—purification, illumination, and union. What are they referring to? Of course he is referring to this process of regeneration, of which Böhme is a culmination. And I think that this is why the West is falling apart. Because I think what happened to Christianity is it lost this process and became entranced with theologies, and hyper-moralism, and all kinds of other things, but it didn't ask people to go through this inner process anymore.

AV: That's, I think, amply born out when you look at the depopulation of the churches. I was traveling recently and saw a church that had been converted into a brewery and this was in Australia.

RF: Happened a lot in England I heard.

AV: Yes, because nobody is going to the church. Well, why are they not going to the church? The population was nominally Christian before, and now it largely has even left that behind and why is that? It's because this process that we're referring to doesn't exist there, so that the light and the life is not present sufficiently to draw people and so that's one of the essential reasons that culturally the West is lost. It's lost because it is literally dis-integrating, and here, I'm not referring to Christianity in the sense that most people refer to it, the way fundamentalists would refer to it or evangelicals would refer to it. It's the *process* we're talking about—*this alchemical process that calls people toward awakening and illumination*—that is what is missing. And that is what integrates at the core of culture, and without that, you don't actually have culture. You can have a society without culture, and I think that's where we're at right now.

RF: Yes, I think that's absolutely true. Exactly, if you don't have that process anymore, you can't have a culture. And you've got what we've got.

AV: Right. The other aspect of that is looking forward, you look into the future, what I could imagine is something that you actually saw in Ireland for example, and really throughout Western Europe, and that was monastic structures. Now monastic structure in itself, just building a monastery or having monks and nuns, is not in itself necessarily the answer. What matters is having centers or places that serve as areas where people can undergo this process and experience what we're talking about and do this kind of work. And that's the source of the living culture and the monastery is of value not only if it has a few manuscripts in it, but also if it serves as a place of storing and conveying what we're talking about.

RF: Yes. And if the monastery is able to send out people who have something to convey back out into Europe.

AV: Right.

RF: This process is so available—all it requires is that one seeks it. Anyone can see and connect with this process; you can be Evangelical, you can be Catholic, you don't even have to be a part of any church. The process is really universal.

AV: It is Christian, but in a very different way than people are accustomed to.

RF: Anyone can open to it. What we're talking about here is the Risen Christ—the risen light and the warm-hearted light and energies within. That's all that the process requires, that one give oneself over to the risen light. So it's not going to offend anyone's sensibility, whether you're saying I'm Christian or I'm not or I can't deal with organized religion. This is still a universal gift.

AV: As happened in the past, people gather together informally or more formally in order to make that process possible, and that's analogous in some ways to what we've seen in the past, sometimes in the really remote past, and again in examples like that of Ireland, but there are others. Because what we're talking about is not formal. It doesn't require a particular formal structure. What it requires is openness to the underlying process and to the goal, the purpose and an understanding of the great metaphysical context of everything that we're talking about—that all those things are necessary and the formal part, the formal structure, and those kinds of things are not necessary in the same way and they may be conducive, but really what we're talking about is a rediscovery of what is present within the whole range of this tradition and is ultimately universal.

RF: Yes and it gets exactly back to what we were talking earlier about with freedom. In other words, what it comes down to is that you are ultimately free to use this Christic warm-hearted process or not. Every human being can do it. Every human being, no matter how sophisticated or how simple, can invite the Warm-hearted One into themselves to work. I do no more than say "Come Lord Jesus, come" and then let go and let the mind sink down, but the whole process is just so open to all and that's where that truth of freedom comes from. You can either decide to undergo it or say no and then just inherit whatever you become, but the choice rests in your freedom.

AV: That's a perfect place to end.

CHAPTER SIX

Preparing for Our Death

Robert Faas (RF), Arthur Versluis (AV)

AV: We've mentioned in passing the subjects of dying, death, and the afterlife, and it seems as though it would be a good idea to have a conversation in which we look more deeply at those, because, of course, they're universal. Everyone experiences death. Everyone has to face that experience and it's something that in our society, we really have no preparation for. In conventional forms of Christianity, it's a matter of people having faith or believing in something, but there aren't practices and there isn't really preparation for it in a profound sense. And so the first question I would have is: how do we prepare for death in this tradition that we've been talking about? What is the preparation for death and how do we approach it?

RF: The only viable way, really, is engaging in a spiritual process in our life in the here and now. This is what Böhme talked about as the Christ process, the process of regeneration. But how can we prepare for death if we don't have any process for the transformation of our own individual self? I think that really is the question, especially for the modern, because what's almost lost totally in the wasteland is that there's no taking care of the soul anymore. And if there's no taking care of the soul, there's no preparation for death.

AV: So really this topic, in many respects, ties together everything that we've talked about. It all leads into this and points toward it. At the very beginning of our conversations, we talked about the nature of developing the soul and nurturing the soul and how our society doesn't really value or present opportunities for that or encourage that, but through art and through literature and philosophical and religious texts, looking at dreams and recognizing the nature of dreams, all of those things are actually preparation for the next life, as well as for the richness of this life. What we're doing is nurturing the soul and the life of the soul. That's developing an inner life. And in addition to that, when you're referring to hesychastic practices—

RF: Purifying meditative practices—hesychasm, experiencing the quiet and the light.

AV:—that is also strengthening and nourishing and illuminating the soul and inner life.

RF: Yes. And the absolutely necessary reality of purifying the soul—the cleansing of the soul—the unburdening of the soul was much more viable before, and many of them got corrupted of course, but fundamentally almost all of the myths and religious literature and early Christianity was very much in dealing with the idea that we need to, in this life and after, in the next life, engage in a process of refinement, of purification, and unburdening ourselves from all of these things we cling to. Whereas modern life does nothing but accumulate.

AV: We all experience that when there's a death in the family, for example, a spouse. It's a subject that's quite close because my father died a couple of years ago and we're still dealing with the accumulation of a lifetime and all of the physical accumulations and he was not a particularly materialistic man, but nonetheless, we bear the burden of our physical accumulations and don't want to relinquish those. And then also, we carry psychological burdens as well as spiritual burdens, so there are different kinds of burdens. Dying before we die is the process, not necessarily of getting rid of these, although that very well may be part of it, but also letting go—I think the process of letting go is a vital part of what we're talking about.

RF: I totally agree. In fact, no purification can happen unless there is an unburdening, unless there's a letting go, and that's another thing that's lost from our Christian history. From the very beginning Christ said—I think it was in the Gospel of John—you have to die before you have another life. Dying to oneself. And early Christianity—all the ways of the Christian initiatory path, which were all about purifying oneself, letting go. Baptism, as you know, is a long practice. It wasn't just a matter of coming in and being baptized. You went through months of becoming attuned and living a different kind of life, so I think again what we have is a lost process—that's nearly at the heart of everything and letting go at the very beginning. I see that in essence as the cross—the sacrificial element that we have to let go of all the things that we cling to and so that we can allow the Christ energies and spiritual light to then begin the process of dissolving and purifying all the different burdens and astraynesses.

AV: I've experienced over the last number of years something that in Ireland is referred to as the veil being thinner—and that's true in Ireland I think for mysterious reasons. I really can't say why Ireland is this way and I don't think it's this way necessarily for the Irish themselves most of the time in the modern era.

RF: Not anymore.

AV: No, not any more, but the way we think of or understand the afterlife is also connected to what we're talking about, because for probably most people, there's just an assumption of there being a wall between this world and anything else or oftentimes, people will believe that there is absolutely nothing on the other side as it were. Whereas my own experience has been that there is continuity—that there is transparency or greater transparency between the physical world that we live in and the afterlife. Assumptions of materiality are not the only way to understand the nature of the world around us, and there is continuity between life as we're talking about it in terms of biology and the material world, and the afterlife—in reality, there's transparency between the two. It's just that we don't recognize it for the most part. It's present, but not visible to us unless we have the eyes to see it and to experience it.

RF: Yes. And I would just add that unless we begin a practice and do the work of thinning the veil through the process of transformation, letting go of our burdens, letting them become transformed, this doesn't happen. There are different ways of one could say having a practice in which the veil between this world and the other are being actively dissolved so that the other world becomes gradually a little more accessible.

AV: Oftentimes people will think of spiritual practice in the inner life as not directly connected to death—or dying and death. Whereas actually it's practiced for that and simultaneously, as we're becoming more attuned to inner life and to allowing the illumination to happen, at the same time, the other world is more present. Is that how you would describe it?

RF: Yes. That the other world is always there within us and it's just that the clouds of our mind—the barriers of our mind, all of the ways that we have accumulated things, form this kind of—until it's dissolved—almost impenetrable barrier because the Christ light and energies are working but we're not able to see that. And that was of course one of the major purposes for Christ's harrowing and also for instituting the sacramental existence, the dissolving of those barriers and reuniting us. And here's where Schelling's *Clara* is a magnificent book about the whole theme of the reuniting of this world and the other world, the spirit world and the nature world, and how one has to become a bearer of the higher light. This is one of the amazing statements in *Clara*, and in this case he meant the light of the Risen Christ, which is exactly the same thing that the hesychasts are talking about: God-created light. There is a real connection between the deeper things in Eastern Christianity and the deeper things in Western Christianity and the journey of the soul.

AV: One of the things that we also don't often hear about is related to what you're talking about, and that is the potential for assisting others—that that's part of what we're talking about as well. The process of inner practice, inner life, and illumination is also not only for ourselves, it's also for others and that's inherent in Christ's sacrifice. There are examples of this that go outside what we normally think might be possible, and I'm thinking here of Johann Gichtel, who was a theosopher—a theosophical practitioner in the tradition of Böhme, and he writes at length about his work on behalf of others—someone who died—that he through his inner struggle, inner practice was able to help someone in the afterlife. A lot of times, there is an assumption in what we could call conventional Christianity that the afterlife is just binary. There's heaven and hell and that's pretty much it. The majority of Christians believe that, whereas someone like Gichtel through his practice, was able to, he said, help others after death and I wondered what you had to say about that.

RF: I think that's absolutely true. I remember reading, I'm not sure if it's exactly what you're referring to, but just a remarkable story about Gichtel, who had a friend who had committed suicide. And then Gichtel talked about how for a year he went to the other realm and was bringing the Christ light in to his friend and he said that in the beginning, when he encountered his friend, it was just a little world of darkness in

145

which he was all shriveled up and in some kind of cold lifeless way of being. And that for hours he would be with his friend every day and gradually began to help the friend undergo a purification and guide him into the light—in a theosophical process of regeneration until finally at some point, he said that his friend finally became like an unbelievably bright light shining star that then ascended into a heaven-world—the deep light world, but only after his help for a long time could that be possible—to help the friend towards that. That's just a remarkable instance of helping someone.

AV: That is one of the stories I was referring to, and Gichtel is really quite remarkable in that regard in that he is one of the few who offers these autobiographical accounts of his own experiences in this process that we're talking about. You can see aspects of it in Böhme. Böhme is not autobiographical in the way that Gichtel is, and that provides a different perspective on the afterlife or aspects of an afterlife. In this particular case, it was helping that particular friend of his, and that's an application of Böhme's understanding and the way that Böhme showed, which was really a synthesis of so many different traditions and currents that come together in this remarkable way to present a path that includes not just practice for oneself, but practice for others. I know I experienced, after my father died, and after a number of different deaths in my life, but particularly after my father died, I had these experiences in dreams, not necessarily only in dreams—of his continuity after death, but not in the kind of simplistic way of him continuing the way I remembered him. It's true that at the very beginning, I had dreams and images of him as a younger man, but there are different kinds of continuity, and what we're talking about is not continuity in the way that we might think of it. I think our concepts and the kind of assumptions that we have in this physical world—we want to carry those along and that's a part of the burden that we carry, actually, because my observation is that there is continuity, but it's not quite the same as we might assume because the other world is—if you want to put it that way—it has different, I want to say laws or rules, but that's not quite right. It's a different dimension than the one that we're in and that changes things, and so I think we need to drop some of our assumptions as part of this process. That's an automatic part, as you experience and as you have experience of others' deaths and what happens after, it compels us to drop some of our preconceptions and to just be open without really expecting—but to be open to communication. That's the word that I wanted to use. That there is actually communication between us and those who have gone before, or at least there can be.

RF: Yes, that communication and communion is truly possible and I would certainly share it and I think you know it, from the very beginning,

147

when [our son] John was lost, the very first day, I had an experience that was completely sponta- neous of the loss: "Oh my God, John is gone. He's dead." But his presence within me was so strong and it said, "No, I'm not dead, dad. I'm in the other world, but I'm not dead." And that was the communication and it has remained— to this present moment—has remained with me. Basically, always I can feel his presence. There are a few times that I can see his face, which is more radiant and that's like a light right be- tween my eyebrows there and I can see his face come forward. And then—so sometimes I will see him. It's not a lot, but every now and then— and it won't last too long, but I know that we are present to one another. That's always there, and there is no talking together in the sense that we talked together before, but there is certainly a communion and a steady presence.

AV: And that communion is also itself part of the process. It's not separate from it or a byprod- uct. It's part of it because we're in a shared en- deavor.

RF: Yes and I don't think that it would be possi- ble—like what John and I had—or what the ex- periences are for me—except that John and I be- gan the light-process or practice when he was about nine, and so we used that process to- gether for many years. He engaged in this prac- tice all of his life and in fact in our final conver- sation, he was talking about how he was on that

148

deployment and said that he was able to do two times a day, when he really had time to engage in this alchemical process. And I think the years of doing that together and individually really resulted in the ability to experience his presence after he moved to the other side.

AV: That is I think rare—it's rare for father and son, or husband and wife, or people who are related in that way to share those kind of practices but what I also would say is there is also a sense in which we share—and this was what the Gichtel story was also about—we share in some sense with everyone who's engaged in the practices of the inner life and illumination. They are in some sense, part of a family as well in that we're all engaged in the same general direction and in that sense, we're all—whether we use the term "family" or use some other term—we're connected in a way that otherwise would not be possible. I'm reminded that there's a novel by Charles Williams in which you don't realize that the narrator, the main character is actually dead and experiencing life, as an observer without being engaged in it, and there's a disconnect there in the sense that that individual is to some extent lost. In fact, I would suggest that if you are interested, the novels of Charles Williams are definitely worth looking at. But the point I'm making is that you use the word "communion"—and there is a sense in which by virtue of what we've been talking about in these conversations, that kind of communion is possible, as is the shared endeavor that someone like Gichtel was referring to. He wrote about that friend, but also other theosophers, Thomas Bromley for example in his *Way to the Sabbath at Rest*, also referred to inner communion. Pordage wrote about this and that's one of the great values of Pordage's work is that he opens doors that otherwise no one opens. And all of these works have to do with what I'm referring to as shared endeavor and you're referring to with the word "communion," and I wondered what you would have to say about that.

RF: I just think that's really at the heart of it. About Charles Williams I recall, didn't he call it co-inherence? Because communion is kind of a dialogical process—the communion between others, but—so I think this communion is at the essence of the process of transformation. That as one is undergoing these refinements and purification, the openness to the other and the other to oneself. And it's a process of being transformed to becoming more and more open, so that one isn't in some sort of self-enclosed cell. That they are open to this world and the other world, the communion between this, the communion with people here, communion with people on the other side, their communion with us—that it basically establishes that there exists a world of communion. This all exists on the spiritual level. I think the other person we have to talk about, again with that is Schelling. His letters—after the loss of his wife and his writing to others—and one of his friends lost his wife also—are utterly remarkable about the degree of communion that you can see that he's experiencing. Most people, particularly academics, are talking about Schelling as a philosopher. You don't really ever hear about the human existential person who was undergoing these experiences after his loss and experiencing communion with the other side, and people that he loved there, and that he was in that communion with them.

AV: That's because the preconceptions that most people have, and certainly in the academic world would have is that someone like Schelling is a philosopher in the sense of abstract philosophizing as it were, using pure rational constructs only. And that's not the case at all. Actually, Schelling was really remarkable. In many respects I think he embodies everything that we've been talking about from the very beginning. For example, Schelling was not closed to the ancient Mysteries. He recognized that there is continuity between the ancient Mystery traditions, which he explored in, for example, an essay on Samothrace and the Christian mysteries. He held that there is continuity between these Mystery traditions. That it's not an opposition. For that alone he is remarkable, but then he also is in the theosophical tradition—the Böhmean tradition—and he's not let's say just in a limited way pulling from it intellectually, but he actually is living it and in some sense, the death of his wife intensified that because of the anguish of the loss—that also opened up what you're referring to and that's why Schelling is I think largely misunderstood and not recognized. Typically, it's very rare to find any allusion to what he's really about and what he's *really* about is what we're discussing.

RF: Yes. He was a practitioner of this Christic way of the light and being in both worlds—just as Böhme was. So he's much more of a practitioner as a person than he is a philosopher. The heart of his life was to be this way, and you can see it quite plainly in his letters and what he alluded to and in *Clara*—at some point Clara talks about, which is really Schelling speaking, how after the death of a loved one, you don't want to just simply return to the ordinary world. If you're really open and grounded in the light, you're in both worlds and you're in communion, and you want to be there for a while and that's not an isolation. It's a way of being that is this continuity that you're talking about and both the departed and the living are still living life together—a relationship is going on. Just as I believe certainly yours was with your dad. Every time we are in communion with the loved ones, we are in relationship with them and it is continuing. It's not a dead relationship.

AV: That's what Schelling really underscores and demonstrates and it also, I think, might tie to the fact that there was a period in Schelling's life when he didn't really publish that much and he wasn't particularly concerned about a university post. He went through fallow periods and those periods were also connected to what we're talking about here—that sometimes it's necessary to let go of aspects of the outer life— the life in the world in order to make possible what we're talking about and that's not necessarily monastic. I'm not talking about monasticism, although that's a possibility.

RF: Exactly. In fact, it's a real opening that the ordinary world and all of its distractions doesn't really know anything about, so it's a calling away to a higher way of being in which you may need solitude, but you also have dialogue. Schelling—he was in both worlds. He needed that solitude to be there in both worlds, but he also was continuing to see his friends, and those letters are remarkable—the communication and the communion that was happening between him and his friends. It's a truly dialogic reality, living differently, rather than the basically foolish way of just completely, no matter what happens to you, just continuing to throw yourself into the world.

AV: In that sense, what we're talking about is dialogic—we're actually engaged in a dialogue and that a lot of what we're discussing is also dialogic—that's a different aspect of what we're describing and discussing, but it's important to recognize that because the dialogue—what we're referring to as dialogic—is also an aspect of communion. We have different backgrounds and different experiences, but we bring those together in to our conversation—in to our dialogue and that itself is an expression of what you're referring to as also communion. And that's true more broadly, so Schelling, writing his friends and meeting with them, had exchanges with them. There's a grander sense of what dialogue means—that dialogue is not just—and this goes all the way to Plato, it's not simply repartée, it's strengthening of a shared understanding so that there's a collective sense to it. So Schelling sharing with his friends—and them sharing with him—is part of a collective communion—what would be the term I would want to invent here? I don't want to say communication because that's just a flat word. I want to say communion—communionative dialogic—dialogue is not just repartée, it's actually moving toward a deeper and deeper shared understanding.

RF: Yes, yes, and then when it happens, it's participatory in each raising the other up. Both are raised up by true dialogue. And I think that is the very essence of Christianity that if rightly understood. That's what Christ is saying when he's saying, "I am with you always." Meaning, "I have come to be with you. I will be with you." It's the being-with and if we're with Christ and his light, he is with us, then all of these processes of change happen in that dialogic or being-with relationship with Christ and being in communion. His being raises us up constantly, and so these alchemical processes happen. There is a really intimate relationship between dialogue and the processes of alchemy.

AV: It's common to see death as an end, as a conclusion, and we feel grief and loss, and yet—. We experience these things, and our assumptions are often that there isn't this continuity and this communion. One of the things that we have to let go in all of this is our set of assumptions about what Christianity is, about what death is, about the nature of who we are, about the nature of what's possible, all of those things have to change in order for this to begin to open up and for us to open up to it. So it's very easy for us moderns to lapse into a kind of cynicism or a refusal, and that's true of many people, I think. And what we're talking about is a completely different perspective, a completely different understanding—that's a better word— that requires us first of all, just to be open. Open enough to allow what we're talking about. It's vital in the society in which we live that there is some place where what we're talking about can be expressed and made available to people in a way that they can grasp and understand. I think that's part of the calling inherent in this conversation that we've been having. That through conversation, through dialogue about this, we're not just exploring intellectual topics. We're aiming at opening up and drawing attention to what's possible and not only possible, but as—there's a verse in the New Testament that refers to the one thing needful and that's what we're really talking about. That there is this path that has been almost completely eclipsed and ignored within the Christian and more broadly, within the Western, by which I mean Western-European world and—so we're opening a door to that and saying, "Look, this exists." And even people like Schelling, whom many so-called philosophers see as a philosopher, is actually an example.

RF: Yes, it's so true. For a lack of a better word, I think what we're really involved with is a death of strictly confessionally-based Christianity, and the rebirth of seeking to live within. There is a deeper Christianity that has been lost after centuries of being off course and getting lost in too much theology that nobody could understand. Rather than living this life that we're talking about, rather than living this deeper Christian existence, what we think of as Christianity has gotten removed from the depths of Christianity. It has gotten lost.

AV: And that's why you end up with all these endless scandals in the Catholic Church—and not only in the Catholic Church by the way—and really when I step back and I look at what's happening, I think there are only two likely paths, and one of them is what's happened in Western Europe, which is for the most part,

Christianity is simply disappearing and churches are being converted into taverns or whatever, and demographically, it's just disappearing because of the absence of what we're talking about. So on the one hand, there's what we're discussing—and then on the other hand, there's the disappearance of it and I really believe that that is the kind of ultimately existential choice Christianity is faced with, and has always been faced with. Either this inner path and mystical life returns to it or you have to ask what's the point? Because in the end *that's* the point. There aren't other things that are the point, the inner life *is* the point.

RF: That *is* the point, exactly. Yes. And it's like they have lost tragically the communion with the Risen Christ. And thereby things have become, in many ways, meaningless, and don't give people anything. They have been wayward and off course. And I think what they're being forced into is their own sense of the need for purification, but they might not make it—more organized Christianity, that is.

AV: But what we're discussing and describing here doesn't actually require organized Christianity in the sense of the entire apparatus of the Catholic Church, for example.

RF: No, it doesn't.

AV: Or for that matter to extend it, Protestant ritual structures—those are intended as expressions of what we're describing—both inner practice and then how that is also communion and communionative practice—that that's the point and these other aspects are not the point. They become, as Böhme called them, just stone churches. They are just stone. They are just constructions, and without this inner life, there isn't anything there, but that inner life continues regardless of those other things and it doesn't require them, it's not dependent on them, because it is enduring. It is timeless. It's always there. It's always there regardless of those things. So the demographic decline of Christianity in Western Europe has nothing to do with what we're talking about because what we're talking about is alive, even if there are only two people or four people or eight people, it still is alive in a way that what Böhme called the stone churches, is not alive.

RF: Exactly, I think that's really true. You can be a part of a Christian community and engage in this, or you can be by yourself. In other words, all of the options are open to you that you would want to be there for your own individual self.

AV: Right.

RF: Nothing is required of you for walking this Christic dialogic path. And whatever form you want that to be in the world, that's pretty much up to your own individuality because they say fundamentally the Risen Christ just says, "Just open to me." That's all. I'm here. Let's journey together.

AV: That's a perfect place to close.

CHAPTER SEVEN

Your Quest

Robert Faas (RF), Arthur Versluis (AV)

AV: In our earlier conversations, we've alluded to the idea of the quest without ever really referring to the grail tradition or the grail cycles in mythology and literature. It seems like that would be an important thing to focus on. What is the meaning of the quest in terms of the Western tradition? What's the importance of the quest in terms of the inner life?

RF: I think it's a beautiful thing. The journey that the soul must undergo is the quest, which means going through the underworld, reaching the point of spiritual development, ultimately raising up the world again. I think it's the quintessential Christian story of the whole theme of purification and regeneration.

AV: It's interesting because it is simultaneously Christian and Pagan at the same time, and in *Parzival*, Wolfram von Eschenbach makes sure to include people who are from outside the

Christian world, like Feirefiz, who is connected to Zoroastrianism. The story of Parzival could be understood as the quest of the soul, the soul's journey through these different essentially dreamlike experiences. Because the story of Parzival is often really dreamlike as a narrative, and the story actually begins and ends to some extent with the suffering of the King, Anfortas. Parzival fails at the beginning because he has to ask the question, and of course quest and question are connected. But what's the meaning of the suffering of Anfortas—the suffering of the grail king and the need to ask this question? What's the inner meaning of that, how the Parzival quest begins?

RF: I believe that would be that he has gone astray and as a result of going astray, entered into the fallen condition. In Böhme's terms, instead of his soul undergoing the trials of the light and continuing to develop and evolve, he gave over to the woundedness of the fallen condition; he became wounded as we all are. It's another way of saying fallen. Because once one loses the paradisiacal condition and one comes into the wounded condition, ultimately one is in need of raising up again from that condition, because nothing worldly can cure it. Nothing—let's say he goes through all the medicines of the world, he'll still find that ultimately the only thing that can bring healing to him is the question and the regeneration that follows. That's brought by Christic love and light, the only things that ultimately can bring healing.

AV: Parzival arrives and he doesn't ask the question. And in not asking the question, essentially, he's not recognizing what's wrong and he's not recognizing the suffering of the king.

RF: Exactly, exactly. What is the question?—the question is the question of love. What ails you? Where are you going—where are you going to? In other words, it's like a therapeutic question. It's a question of a love therapy and the asker of the question becoming kind of like a co-sufferer. There is a great theme throughout Orthodoxy and Western Christianity about suffering with the other, and that's the whole thing that he did not do. He didn't ask the question of the co-suffering.

AV: No, and because he didn't ask that question, then all of these other adventures and other parts of the story take place, and he has to go through what's almost like a dream-sequence in order to return—he has to go through all of these different chapters and adventures until finally he can return and he's in a position to do that.

RF: Yes, I think that's absolutely true. In other words, it is an alchemical quest. He has to go through the nigredo, and all those adventures and strange things are journeys through the underworld of the soul in which he has to overcome evil and become purified and transformed, and so I think the most apt way to describe this is the alchemical quest.

AV: Alchemy is even alluded to in the Parzival narrative and alchemical colors play a role: black, white, and red.

RF: Yes, the three stages.

AV: They recur throughout the text. So there clearly is an alchemical coding in the grail narrative, focusing here mainly on Parzival, because it's the most elaborate and most complete of the different grail stories. And it's interesting too. There is a part where Parzival in his quest meets Trevrizent the hermit and a lot of the narrative—

RF: On Good Friday.

AV: Exactly. So he meets this hermit on Good Friday. A lot of the narrative is about courtliness and courtly life and male/female relationships and we can go into that, but then you have these other characters. In the case of Trevrizent the hermit, there is no male/female relationship in the same way. And actually Anfortas also, but that's something maybe we can talk about later. Trevrizent the hermit is an initiatory figure. He's initiating Parzival, I think.

RF: Yes, into the deepest Christian mystery.

AV: Into the mystery of—

RF: Of regeneration, redemption, and because Good Friday, of course, goes into Easter. And so I think it's the highest Christian mystery that he's being initiated into.

AV: If I remember right, it's also during that time that he discusses the grailstone. I think the grailstone comes in during that conversation and the grailstone itself is directly connected to the Christian mystery of regeneration and redemption because the grailstone is such a mysterious symbol. People think of the grail as this chalice and there are these sometimes essentially ridiculous theories that have been propagated about the chalice grail in terms of very materialistic arguments about heredity bloodlines and this and that.

RF: Crazy, yes.

AV: It's fantasy. But then you look at the grailstone, which actually is a stone, it's a clear stone. So it's lucid. Light passes through it, a really mysterious symbol and it's more mysterious the more you look into it.

RF: Yes, so truly, and in the Apocalypse [Revelation of John], we read that to he who overcomes and becomes imbued with the light, I will give a white stone, and what's more, it says that we are meant to become fiery stones. What do those things mean? Here we are at the highest Christian mysteries, and there are so many allusions to this mysterious stone. Christ is the stone. The Risen Christ is the stone.

AV: Right. The stone rolled away is also significant.

RF: Yes.

AV: I think in terms of Apocalypse, you're referring to the Revelation to John.

RF: Yes, exactly.

AV: Yes.

RF: And that mystical chronology. There are so many things in there about the higher grail mysteries.

AV: Right, so the Book of Revelation is an opening into what we see developed in the grail tradition. Most people wouldn't be aware of that connection between the Book of Revelation and the Grail tradition, but actually, they're both very dreamlike and hieratic. So that the journey through the grail world—we accept that it's a real world, but real in the sense that we accept that a dream is real. And I think that aspect is tied to Revelation because the dream, the revelation that we're talking about here, is a metaphysical revelation. It's not only cosmological, there's a metaphysical dimension and that's why revelation is important here.

RF: Yes, I think that's so true, and I think we can liken the journey in those dreamlike states to the afterdeath journey—going through the processes of purification in the realm of the refining fire. And so that there's a real parallel there and I'm sure it's not by accident what the knight goes through is really what the soul goes through in its journey in the afterdeath state to reach transfiguration.

AV: I want to explore that, but I don't want to leave the mystery of the grailstone quite yet, because it appears as a clear stone—the names of those who are connected with it appear on it in this kind of invisible writing that appears and then disappears. So there's a kind of annunciation—a sort of destined quality—Parzival is destined.

RF: Yes, and again, that connects with the Apocalypse—because in Revelation we read that I will give a new name. Because as well as receiving the lightstone, one is also given a new name. No one knows the name, but one has to go through this process and achieve before that new name is granted to one.

167

AV: Which is a way of alluding to transfiguration.

RF: Yes, yes.

AV: And mystery of transfiguration. The other thing is that the stone—the grailstone provides food and drink in a mysterious way, which connects to the mysteries of Christ because one of his miracles, of course, was to provide food and drink, so there's yet another allusion.

AV: Yes, and that refers also to the Eucharistic element. The bread and wine. And the souls feeding from the light-body of Christ. We can remember all of the things that Böhme talks about in that regard, so that one develops a new body—from the light-body of Christ. We become new beings, grow a new light-body.

AV: So the mystery of the grailstone manifesting food and drink is also connected not only to the Eucharist, but to new body, to the body of light, to transfiguration, but none of this is made explicit in the text. In other words, the story reads as a story, and yet at the same time, all of these elements are woven into it almost invisibly—they're there to glimpse and discover. The grailstone really is a grailstone and it really is what we're talking about, but at the same time certain things are left unsaid so that we as readers or as hearers of the story can fill in the blanks as it were and come to understand it for ourselves.

RF: Yes it asks us to become intuitively connected, which through story as we know—and
myth—it's much easier for us to work with
those intuitively, than everything being an intellectual process. I think the story in that mode
awakens the heart and its intuitiveness to be
able to then grasp also what's not being said,
but it knows what is said through the imagery.

AV: There are other things that are also said explicitly and I'm thinking here of book nine
where Kyot, the Provençal—and that's significant too, because there's this Provençal tradition, which is where the Cathars are of course,
but it's where the Troubadour tradition was
very strong and the tradition of courtly love and
so the whole region of Provence is significant.
Kyot the Provençal is actually said to be the origin in some ways of the narrative of Eschenbach, but there is this reference in there to keeping the stone secret until the time is right. The
stone is also referred to (and no one has really
explained or understood—there are just theories about this) with the mysterious phrase "lapsit exillis" which could be *lapis ex caelis* or stone
from the heavens, or stone from heaven. I think
that's actually the most likely—just speaking for
myself, I think it's the most likely way of understanding that, but people are appointed to the
grail. The grail—the *lapsit exillis*, which is mentioned by Eschenbach is tied to the Phoenix—in
the text, to the idea of death and rebirth—the

169

burning to ashes and then rising again, and one thing beyond those is that the stone is also explicitly linked with the neutral angels. There are fallen angels; there was a battle. But there were neutral angels who didn't fight in that battle, and that's what the stone is linked to and I wondered what you think about—what your perspective is on that because it seems to me really significant in a number of ways that the grailstone is linked to neutral angels.

RF: I think the connection is analogous to Dante's first circle. I think there you find the neutral angels. That's their place, if I'm remembering correctly in *Inferno*. And those who do not, in a sense, take sides, or remain always on the fence—neither going really to the left nor right—to the dark nor the light—or always are sort of left in this suspended state in which they can never become anything. And so that I think their only possibility or connection is that they must finally ask the question too. They must finally make a choice. They must finally elect for the stone or for the journey, for the quest. Otherwise they will never become anything and that's even worse than if you're in the dark place because you've got a chance of maybe at some point getting out of there, so to speak.

AV: So the grailstone in this context would be the cosmic choice. It represents this cosmic turning point, which is also stone. It's the hardest. It's the most material substance and yet, it's exiled from heaven, and—so it penetrates—heaven penetrates to the depths you could say and the stone symbolizes that also.

RF: Yes. And it's kind of like the philosopher's stone in that it's a stone, but it's also waxy—in other words it's kind of malleable too, but it's still hard. So it has the qualities of the opposites united and raised up.

AV: And it's also linked to the light of the stars.

RF: Yes, to the high astral.

AV: There are all these different aspects that are embedded in this or captured in this extraordinary image and symbol.

RF: There really are. And it reminds me that one of the people that actually did write about some of this was Carl Jung, who explored the stone as well as the grail. And in fact his wife wrote a significant book on the grail. She was a great student of the grail, and she and Marie von Franz collaborated together to write a book on the grail. But Jung had significant things to say about the stone and related matters in some of his alchemical works. There are three or four volumes that are devoted to his alchemical work.

AV: I can see that, because Jung was drawn to all these kinds of traditions. I don't always put a lot of stock in the interpretation or spin that he subjects them to.

RF: Nor do I. I think he psychologizes too much ultimately in many cases, takes them out of their deeper spiritual reality.

AV: Which is beyond the individual. That's what we draw from the symbolism of the grail-stone itself. It's beyond the strictly human—the fact that I'm referring to a dream journey and how we experience the grail story doesn't mean that I'm reducing it only to strictly an individual. Ultimately, the individual quest has cosmological and metaphysical dimensions that are beyond who we are as individuals and I do agree with you. I think that's where Jung tended too much to limit what he was writing about and also to sometimes invert or distort the meaning of what he was working with. Sometimes he would invert cosmology or metaphysics for his own purposes, but yes, I think Jung's great virtue was opening the door to all this material for so many people.

RF: Yes, absolutely, without doubt he was a door-opener. He just opens the door to alchemy—the grail, all of these deep archetypal stories and truths that did survive in the East, while clearly the whole Western tradition was being utterly lost. Jung pointed to it and started to explore it.

AV: I think that is still having an effect—Jung having done that—especially after the release of the *Red Book* and its extraordinary imagery. All of that is still to be worked through culturally. And the significance of these great inheritances that we have from the Western tradition—alchemy, esoteric dimensions of Christianity, the Christian Mysteries connected to the ancient Mysteries. These are things we've been exploring, you and I, for a very long time, but when we look at society as a whole, it's as if they almost don't exist. There are only a few places where they peek out into larger consciousness and Jung happens to be one of those places. But I want to come back to something in the grail story. There's another aspect to *Parzival* and that is the role of women in Parzival story and in the grail tradition because in the West, more broadly in Western tradition going back millennia. You can see even in Julius Caesar when he was writing about the tribes of Britain how the women would fight. The importance of women and the roles of women was very different than what you see in, for example the Islamic world or the other parts of the world. The role of the women in the West going back very, very far is just different than it is elsewhere and by West, I mean Western Europe. You see this in the grail tradition, and I just wanted to sketch just in the case of Parzival, the female characters that are important because you've got Herzeloyde, who is Parzival's mother. You've got Sigune, who is his advisor; she's advising as the tale goes along. And then Condwiramurs he ends up marrying; she becomes his wife. So there are these three pivotal female characters in the quest and then there's a fourth, Cundrie, and Cundrie is this kind of prophetic hag-figure who recurs periodically and she excoriates him, and she's prophetic and enigmatic and hideous, frightening, so you've got all of these different female roles that are really vital as a part of a grail cycle. I wondered what you would have to say in terms of thinking about the role of women in this grail and alchemical tradition that we're looking at.

RF: I think it's probably the deepest and truest representation of woman that exists. In other words, if we go back biblically to before the fall, and when Adam and Eve were joined together in union as the angelic couple. Böhme had man as the fire spirit, woman as the light spirit, and so the very essence of woman, especially in her raised-up condition, is to be a conveyer of the light, which I think has great grail implications. The carrier of the light: and here we have the grail maidens who are carrying the light or carrying the grail. And so it opens up this dimension of woman and I think her deepest, truest role as well as some fallen roles where there's the fallen element and then Cundrie—ultimately, she's striving and, in the end, she does undergo the changes.

AV: Cundrie—she has an important role. I'm not sure she's symbolizing the fall really fits it because she has this kind of prophetic role. She has an archetypical role in the drama and she's needed in the drama actually to play that role. And so there's a fated or a destined quality to the role she's playing and to these other roles, the maiden, the grail maiden, like Repanse de Schoye, a princess—sometimes she's referred to as queen, but she has to be pure because the stone is itself described as the perfection of paradise.

RF: Yes and it's not necessarily that it's a sexual purity, but the pure being—she's reached the point of having become entirely purified and can receive the light and the grail. I think you're right. It isn't just the fallen-ness with Cundrie, but it's that when woman fell, she entered into kind of a dual role. On one side, she, like Adam, had these fallen elements in which she could become a torment to man. Her other side was that she was meant to lead man back to the quest—back to the proper way, so she had more of a dual element to her and I think that absolutely what you're saying is very true about kind of a dual aspect to Cundrie.

AV: That's right. That's what I was trying to point to: it's not the case that she's only negative. There's a positive dimension. It's manifested in a way that is alarming and disturbing, but it is not negative in the sense that it points in the wrong direction. It actually points in the right direction.

RF: Yes, she's almost like a conscious goad.

AV: Exactly.

RF: A conscious striking back at us—you fall, get back on course. You're in this ridiculous direction and I'm going to keep kicking you in the ass until you wake up.

AV: That's right and it's interesting and I'll just interject this because a lot of what we're talking about is really analogous to Tantric traditions in India or in Asia where again, someone like Cundrie is from an external perspective, "bad" or "a hag", but actually, a deeper look at this figure or the women characters more broadly is that they are vital to the quest itself and—

RF:—and trying to help man raise himself up.

AV: Right and that they're also part of that raising up—that regeneration. The female characters, including even Cundrie.

176

RF: Yes, yes. She's—exactly. She's like a conscious figure that helps keep him going to get on to the right direction.

AV: Right.

RF: And then like you're saying with the Tantric aspects, well I think that's so true, but it's like the Christian Mystery of higher eros that I think especially is reflected in—remember the marriage finally between Parzival and Condwiramurs, what happened? There was a sword between them for three days after they were married. Now that's a very mysterious thing, but if one understands this history, that's like the three days where you don't really come together fully until you are purified enough, like three days in a tomb, and those three days were when each, the man and the woman, in a sense has to undergo the process of the purification of his or her eros so that when the two do come together erotically and sexually, it's as truly transfigured, purified beings that are then on the path of a higher eros. So in the end the Christian mystery is not a denial of eros at all. It's a transfiguration of eros and I think that's what's in the *Parzival*.

AV: That brings us back to what I was alluding to earlier with Kyot, the Provençal and the importance of the courtly love tradition, which I thought we would come back to and in fact we have, because it's woven into this chivalric story of Parzival. The courtly love tradition—the tradition of the Troubadours, the tradition of the man in service and I wouldn't over emphasize it, but it's in celibate service to the Queen. Service to the noble women is a deep and abiding tradition within Western Europe and especially in this area of Provençe, and that's distinctively Western and it is what you're referring to as tradition of higher eros—of eros transformed.

RF: And I think in the *Parzival*, it's taken a step beyond. That courtly tradition was so powerful, but it didn't get beyond the idealization of women. It didn't come into true union between two equals that are in a sense, able to transform together and that then can enter the highest mystery. But the Parzival does. There is a full union—spirit, soul, and flesh—between the two of them.

AV: There is and it's interesting that—and I hadn't noticed this before, there is also a tradition of the grail king being celibate and Anfortas—

RF: He's wounded in the genitals.

AV: Right, so that's like a reverse or a dark version, but actually for the grail king, celibacy also plays a role in what we're talking about. That it's an aspect of the transcendence of the fallen.

RF: Yes and I think the problem with the celibacy—is that it became like a physical celibacy, which then end up like the neutral angel—that if you don't have an understanding of what celibacy is meant to be, which is for a while during that period, to use the celibacy to undergo the inner transformation of the lower elements of the sexuality or passion so that they can become merged or transformed and then merged with love and then you have finally the union of love and passion together, which practically no one has ever been able to do. But I think these things point to that. And then—and that's why I think that final marriage in *Parzival* is rare. It really entered into a full higher eros that included the flesh. He was no longer celibate, but they went through a mysterious celibate three days. And I think it might be worth-considering also Wagner's *Parsifal*, where he includes a lot of these sexual elements; and remember the story of Klingsor, the evil magician. He has to face the temptations of the flesh again, where most others fall. And that's where Klingsor fell, but Parzival didn't fall. So he went on to a higher state.

AV: But Klingsor did fall.

RF: Klingsor did definitely fall, yes.

AV: Yes, that's so interesting because he's this negative figure showing what can happen from a different perspective.

RF: Yes and in history that's what's so interesting. He was one of these esteemed knights on the way and then along the way he didn't make it, and he fell instead and so then became literally the embodiment of the dark element of things and realized that.

AV: And he was also celibate in a different way, which is—I think the text has it that he was smooth down below, which is a way of alluding to emasculation.

RF: But he had been emasculated; he became impotent. Like it says about the satanic figure and his fall. The same thing happened to him.

AV: Yes—Klingsor is emasculated, in some sense given over to evil. The story of Parzival is I think extraordinary and moves towards this transcendent ending—culminating in the marriage of Parzival and Condwiramurs, but then also with the expectation that Parzival will himself become the grail king.

RF: Yes and she will become the grail queen and they will become the grail couple.

AV: Which again is alchemical.

RF: Which again is alchemical.

AV: And one thing that I didn't want to overlook in thinking about this is that we're also talking about a grail landscape. We haven't alluded to that, but in the text itself, there are references I was interested to see because I see it in a different way, having been to so many of these places, there's specific reference to Brittany, to England, meaning Western England especially because there's this esoteric link between Cornwall and Brittany—western coasts of both of those countries, and then Ireland. And there's a real grail region in Western France, Brittany, in the area around Barenton and I've also been to Tintagel, which is the birthplace of Arthur, and it's very commercialized, but behind that, it's real. There is something genuinely there and certainly that's the case in the area in Brittany around Barenton and the Fountain of Barenton and that whole region, which is so closely connected to Merlin and the aspects of the grail tradition, the Valley of No Return, all of these different landscape dimensions of what we're talking about are very much alive. The grail cycle is not purely historical or antiquarian. It's actually deeply embedded in the actual landscape of Western Europe and it's still alive. It's enduring as this living tradition, so as soon as you're in touch with it, it's in touch with you.

RF: Yes, the true spirituality of it is breaking through and even in the Earth, and the land, and as you say, which I think ultimately is part of the reason for the grail cycle's very existence. And I think the grail is the carrier of that rebirth or regeneration, and it's meant to evolve into the holy Earth—the Earth of light. And those places were saturated with that in that time, and still are.

AV: That's right and it's simultaneously beyond place, but also embedded in place. And in landscape and in transformed landscape, transfigured landscape.

RF: Yes, visible windows into eternity.

AV: I think that's right. So if we're thinking about the grail tradition today, for people who are engaged in seeking and in their own quests, what's the importance—what's the meaning of the grail cycle and the grail traditions and mythology you could say—although I'm not sure that's quite the right word—for people today if we're going to sum up what the importance of this is, how would we do that?

RF: I think a couple of ways. The first thing that comes to mind is maybe we need to read Eliot again with new eyes, because he accurately captured so much with the wasteland and the failure of modernity, and it's all about the grail.

We've fallen into the modern wasteland—the modern person has fallen into becoming the hollow man, and we're living in the wasteland. I don't know anything that could be truer. So I think Eliot's words help us to put it in a modern perspective and that also I think that there could be a new grail story for the present that begins with the idea that we are in the wasteland. The question wasn't asked and here's where we are and here's where it's possible to come to again. Kind of like a re-igniting of the quest. And I think we're very thirsty for someone to write a new story of the new grail so to speak.

AV: I think connected with that—it's on the one hand that we're in a wasteland meaning in a fragmented condition.

RF: We're all shot to hell right now.

AV: The world in a diminished state—we broadly don't really have culture in that kind of deep sense that does exist in the grail tradition and so the implications of the grail tradition are not only individual, they're also cultural. They are larger than us. That's why I mentioned the landscape—the landscape is a real landscape and it is alive if you are aware of it. Of course, if you're stumbling along as an obese zombie eating cotton candy from the stand—

RF: Or gobbling drugs, chronic drinking, or whatever.

AV: Or whatever. Then—it might not be open or visible, but it's actually there and there's always the possibility of that being recovered, renewed. There's always the possibility that asking the question in that context is not what ails you as an individual, as this person—but rather, what ails us?

RF: What ails us?

AV: What ails us. And what's the key to healing?

RF: Renewal.

AV: Healing and renewal on a much larger scaler potentially. Of course, it begins with the individual. Parzival is an individual on a quest and we're each individuals and we're each on a quest, but there is this larger context, which in the grail tradition is the kingdom, and the kingdom is in need—the kingdom is disconsolate and in disarray and we're at a place to restore that and our kingdom in our society is in disarray, so the grail I think—the grail cycle, as I'm thinking about it, has cultural significance that goes well beyond only the individual.

RF: Yes, I think that's absolutely true. That only from something like the grail can spring the new culture and then its Christic connection because otherwise, if you don't have that, there is no antidote. It will continue in the horrible dead and even demonic direction, with things gradually falling apart and people becoming more and more like angry machines. And that what's going to be one possible future. The other is if there is a renewal through the grail in the culture—a wholly different culture can be built.

AV: I think that's absolutely true and that is an important, maybe I would say a vital part of what the grail tradition in general, and Parzival in particular, has to share with us is these are keys to a living culture. How to deal with others, chivalric code, esoteric dimensions, alchemical path, a higher—

RF: Higher eros for man and woman.

AV: Higher eros, restoration of how man and woman can be together in a not fallen but transfigured state. All of these things are woven into this tradition, so it's far more than strictly an individualized purely psychological quest that we're talking about. It has much greater scope.

RF: So truly said, yes. Yes it does. It's about the whole—I mean all of existence—but my God, what a culture that would be, based on the grail—what that would look like!

AV: Isn't it a fascinating idea? It existed to some extent and it can exist again in a different form in a different way.

RF: Yes, absolutely. In fact, I really believe that in its nature it's meant to be recast for the time that it's in. Same eternal messages, but recast into the particular time and this is certainly a time that needs it.

AV: It does.

RF: Desperately.

AV: I think the other aspect of this is that it's the very disarray—the woundedness of our own time that makes it so suitable for exactly this kind of turn. And this tradition—I think the possibility is certainly there, but again, it depends on the choices of Parzival and of all the others in order to make what happens at the end of narrative possible. So hence the reason for the individual journey with a much greater significance.

RF: Yes, and bringing to consciousness that for people that there really is a choice that can be made. I think nowadays so many don't even know that there's any kind of choice anymore.

AV: No, I think that's right. There is always a choice. And that's perhaps a good place to draw this to a conclusion for now.

RF: Sounds good, Arthur.

CHAPTER EIGHT

Advice for the Spiritual Seeker

Robert Faas (RF), Arthur Versluis (AV)

AV: We've been talking for some time now about a whole series of different themes and topics and aspects of the Western spiritual path and specifically within that, Christian mysticism understood as a Mystery tradition. And as we think about the journey of the conversations, I wondered whether it might be a good idea to start with in this concluding conversation, a summary or overview of advice for somebody who is a seeker, and then also advice for further practice and how to continue to develop within this tradition that we've been discussing and exploring together. So why don't we start with some thoughts about what to say to someone who's beginning on this path and summarize some of the things that we've discussed?

RF: That sounds like a good start. Let's start by talking to someone who is a seeker and who wants to know where he or she would start in the Western Christian tradition. I think first thing that I would talk to someone about is the need to be awakened or come onto the journey of the soul—come into the whole Mystery process in Christianity that was foreshadowed by or was at least a part of the old Pagan Mysteries—that there is an absolute need for a process. A process of regeneration and the process of rebirth. A psycho-spiritual process that has been, in many ways, eclipsed, but the reality is, you need a way. I would talk to him or her about how you have to have a way. This is not intellectual or cognitive or rational understanding or whatever. It's entering upon a way of the regeneration of one's own being through Christian Mystery—essentially through the Risen Christ.

AV: That's where we started. In the first conversations we were talking about the continuity about the ancient Mysteries and ancient Mystery traditions, which were about regeneration and rebirth.

RF: Yes, absolutely. Metamorphosis.

AV: Descent into the underworld and return. Regeneration. Return to light. Revelation of light. These are the themes of the ancient Mysteries and I remember we talked about Christianity as part of that—as a Mystery tradition itself.

RF: Yes, and originally and still, Eastern Christianity, generally calls the Sacraments the Mysteries. They've always called them that from the very beginning, they were named a Mystery. And so we still have that. Of course, in the West, they become more watered down, and now have kind of gone into an eclipse, but yes, it's always been there. I think in the modern world what we're seeing is almost like the death or at least the overshadowing of it—the losing of it.

AV: What we're talking about is a process that involves our whole being. Of course the intellect is a part of it, because that's part of what makes us who we are, but what we're talking about is something that goes beyond the intellect alone. It involves our whole being and that was part of our conversation with relation to the Mystery traditions, but also to—advice to pay attention to dreams, to recognize that one's dream life is a reflection of and a manifestation of one's inner life and that inner life is not strictly intellectual. It involves who we are as a whole person or as a whole being. And that actually is also an opening, the dream life is an opening into what

191

Schelling called the spiritual world and the metaphysical dimensions of our existence, which in our society, actually are excluded or ignored. We live in a very materialistic society that largely excludes the kinds of things we're talking about and that's why it's so vital to remind people of the existence of these things.

RF: Yes, that there really is a spiritual world and that it has to do with our whole being and our whole destiny—both temporary and eternal. I really believe that we have become, as you say, so materialistic that so many people are just going mad. They can't bear it. You look at the unbelievable use of drugs, heroin, the constant distraction—

AV: Opioids.

RF: —opioids. The constant distraction through the media, many of the new technological things that keep a person's mind completely off track, and in many ways, modern existence has become sort of a spirituality-free vacuum.

AV: And as a result, part of what we were suggesting people do or someone might do—an individual who's a seeker—is read the great works of literature as part of a process of renourishing our inner life. Literature has a role in conveying culture, and culture is really spiritual at heart. And that's part of this larger process, which is an integrative process and it's integrative for us as individuals, but it's also integrative for us with regard to the larger context of what it means to be human and that's where reading the great works of literature, the great works of religious literature are so important, because otherwise our development takes place without reference points and without a sense of direction. And also without richness and that richness comes from having all of these works that help nourish our soul and that's also something that we talked about.

RF: Yes, and couldn't be more well said. Without literature and of course holy scriptures, without that profound literature, you have no sense of human spiritual history at all. It's just like you've wiped out that humanity ever had a spiritual history—a legacy that one desperately needs.

AV: That's actually what happened historically in—to some extent, in the Soviet Union and overwhelmingly within Communist China— once, and then other places as well—Cambodia, for instance. Whenever the extreme Left, the extreme egalitarian Left takes over, driven partly by Marxism and Marxist anti-religious mentality, you have this kind of purging and this purging results in a kind of materialism, which demands that all of these great traditions, including that literature, disappear and that's why you had this true holocaust in Tibet for example.

RF: Yes, that's absolutely true and it disappears and in that disappearance, one of the things that happens is the dark side, as Böhme would call it, the wrath side—just consumes them—these people and inevitably you have these unbeliev-able atrocities. I mean it's a killing frenzy—un-told millions that we know of in China, Cambo-dia, and other places as well, who basically went on in the same way as Russia in terms of obliterating their own history. The wonderful great works were hated by all those people.

AV: There were two Russians who really had—I think—a handle on this and that I would sug-gest somebody read. One is Dostoevsky because Dostoevsky in his character of The Grand In-quisitor captures some of this mentality that you're referring to, which really I think primar-ily resides on the left. I think there's something about the far-left ideology that lends itself to this and Dostoevsky had insight into that and the other is Berdyaev. Berdyaev had direct expo-sure to Communism in Russia. He saw it de-velop and in exile in France, really wrote some of the most penetrating work on what we're talking about and he of course was informed di-rectly by Böhme in the theosophical tradition.

Berdyaev saw—informed by Böhme and Böh-mean theosophy, which he was deeply imbued with and understood, he saw firsthand the ho-mogeneity of the far left, recognized its anti-reli-gious, anti-spiritual, and I think the better term is probably in this context, anti-spiritual nature, and so I was suggesting that someone might read Dostoevsky and Berdyaev for insight into this, but also specifically Berdyaev for under-standing dimensions of this process that we've been discussing because I think he really did un-derstand the theosophical mysteries in a way that very few philosophical figures have.

RF: Yes, he penetrated quite deeply into all of this and it would be very helpful if he would be-come more well-known for this because he rec-ognized essentially just like Dostoevsky that if you really go over to a militant atheism or ni-hilism, then at the same time, you find you've delivered yourself over to the beast, to the dark. And that's why these people always appear ul-timately as killers on a large scale, justifying ev-erything that they do because without religion or God or spirituality, I think you ultimately be-come at the mercy of this wrathful dark element in humanity that they don't even like to say ex-ists. And I think you see vestiges of it in the modern left with their penchant for shouting people down, declaring anybody that doesn't believe like them as just some kind of an evil person. It's the same kind of basic mentality.

Many of them haven't gone that far, but most of them are pretty much God-deniers.

AV: The denial is of the kind of spiritual traditions that really we've been focusing on and the spiritual process. Because what happens—and this is something we talked about before—is people become identified with the external, with the political agenda of transforming the world externally by force and that's what leads to what you're talking about. And people who are on the right, people who are conservative, in general want to conserve. And what they want to conserve are the cultural and political dimensions that are stable and that are conveyed through history. So they want to conserve and tend to be hostile to or very skeptical of ideologies that seek power in order to force other people to conform and transform the world in that way. And that's why there is this kind of underlying dimension, which is not necessarily political in the sense of political parties. What we're talking about here are political tendencies that have spiritual dimensions and I don't think that is said very often. It's largely not part of the conversation, but it needs to be said. And the reason it needs to be said is really what we're talking about is on the one hand, an affirmational perspective, which is affirmational of the great works of humanity and the great potential that we have to become better, wiser, more loving, and on the other hand, one has the opposite.

And so there's a kind of bifurcation, there's a great choice that we have to make and the force within our society right now tends towards the materialistic, toward the left, the extreme left, toward the tearing down and destruction of the old ways. That perspective is hostile to spiritual process and spiritual practice, and we can recognize that. But really, what we're talking about—what we've been talking about is an inner process, which might very well take place in reclusion from society. In other words, we can't solve the world's problems. We're just talking about recognizing the principles that are at work and what we can do is turn toward our own inner life in order to realize more deeply what we've been talking about and I wondered what role would you say psychology plays in this? Because that's also something we talked about, psychology in terms of the process of deeper spiritual life and of illumination. What's the role of psychology or psychological awakening in spiritual awakening?

RF: I think that it's absolutely crucial. And the reason that I say that is many of the directions that we're talking about in materialistic society in a sense, as much as they might talk some about psychology, they don't really follow a psychology of the soul. If you're going to enter into the spiritual path, if you do not have some way psychologically of dealing with and overcoming your past, you will never really develop a regeneration of your being. You will simply carry your burdens along with you very deeply and you will meet them on the other side. So all of the things that happen in your life that may have broken you, were difficult, and that you're still carrying in your relationships, in your ordinary life, if they're not paid attention to on the path, then that's going to be delivered to you with all that intact and waiting in the other world. You simply cannot reach regeneration or without dealing with the psychological—without tending your path, which interestingly enough, if one really looks at all the great works of the past and the works about the other side, all of them are talking about people ending up in all these various states. Why? Because they lived a certain way and they didn't deal with this stuff.

AV: Dante comes to mind here, for example.

RF: Absolutely. People are consumed by their past and acting out their stuff. In the old days, they would have called it sinful. People go in a psychological direction that completely ties the soul up and never deals with the past. Only by facing and beginning to work through that can one become freed to the true processes of cleansing as an essential foundation for transformation. So I don't think there is any true spiritual growth without dealing with the psychological.

AV: And that has to do also with dealing with what Jung called the shadow. That's a term that reflects what you're referring to—the shadow.

RF: Yes, it is the past. The shadow is our undone past.

AV: And we work with that by —

RF: If we do it in the Christic way, we work with that by realizing that one of the Mysteries—the Mystery of baptism—is fundamentally a cleansing of the soul, a purifying. The old mystics gave the name for that purgatorial realm on the other side: the realm of the purifying fire. Böhme alludes to it. Schelling—any number saw that we must go through a fiery cleansing in regard to our psychological burdens and wayward direction. And that the first Mystery of Christianity in a sense, baptism, what we're talking about is the baptism of the soul. Not just the rite, but the cleansing of the soul through the light energies of Christ and the light. It's really a deepening of understanding of what that ancient Mystery—what's usually the first one was—as we know, what? Purification. In a way before psychology, that was the psychology of the soul and this of course is still viable.

AV: What we've also talked about before was the limitations of psychology understood as separate from spirituality. Psychology cut off from spirituality and envisioned as existential or however one wants to term it, is ultimately materialistic. In other words, psychology without a larger spiritual context is not capable of doing what we're talking about. That's why you referred to baptism and the mystery of purification. It's a mystery because it's spiritual. It includes—and emanates from this dimension that is beyond the physical and therefore beyond psychology. That's the key in terms of going beyond our past traumas, our burdens that we carry. The only way we can go beyond these is through mystery. And that and the mystery is the mystery of forgiveness, of love, of light, which is ultimately spiritual, but includes the psychological.

RF: Yes, truly, there is simply no way that both of them are not needed. In other words, "psycho-spiritual" is a wonderful term. We need desperately a psycho-spiritual process that takes both into account and we can't divorce them. Some people just becoming spiritual. Some people just using psychology and behaviorism or approaches like that. The soul can never be regenerated unless it's a psycho-spiritual undertaking.

AV: And that's why in the ancient Mysteries, people underwent a process. They would go into the Mystery experience and there were stages or aspects of that which included terror, which included an emotional range, which is a psychological range so there is a psychological dimension to the mystery process. And it's not only psychological but is has to include the psychological to make possible the awakening process. The illumination process.

RF: Yes, that's so very true and I think that Christ coming—what he did is, after he came, you didn't have to go through these difficult initiation processes that you had to go through in the Mystery before. He, in his coming, he made available the light and the energies of light immediately in a sense to everyone that wanted to come towards them so that you did not have to undergo this tough getting-to. And in reality what he did was bring the mystery of the light and the energy of the light to accessibility so that one really needs to only turn and ask and then undergo the initiatory process. I don't think that's well understood. We could put it this way: in the old Mysteries you had to seek the light. In the new Mysteries with Christ, the light is there for you to enter into it.

AV: And this is something we talked about before, which is understanding Christianity as a Mystery tradition is a vital part of what we've been talking about and introducing.

RF: It absolutely is. And it is a centuries-old mystical tradition, but then so often the people that look back—they look through their own glasses and they don't see the mystery. They might say people believed this or that, or they did this or whatever, but it's all kind of partial aspects, largely missing the fact that the early Mysteries, Christians were involved in a Mystery existence.

AV: This is a good point, I think, at which to start to think a little bit about advice for someone who has gotten to the point of understanding what we're talking about in a deeper way and wants to continue and deepen the process. What would your advice be to that person who is engaged in the spiritual process we're discussing? What are the things to watch out for, the things to look for, what are some suggestions that you'd have for somebody who's engaged in this psycho-spiritual process of awakening?

RF: I think the first thing I would say is that the good news is that it is true that if you ask, you shall receive. In other words, to demystify, to have an understanding that to step onto this path, it is not difficult. To continue on may be difficult, but the stepping on to it through Christ was made relatively simple. So that first thing to—I would talk about it in a two-fold way—that only two things are necessary. And the first is the invocation, calling on Christ to come enter the soul—to come into one. "Come, Lord Jesus, come." Which is actually in the Scripture at the closing. It's called the hesychastic heart-prayer and that's exactly what it ends with is "Come, Lord Jesus, come." So it's first calling Christ to be with one and bring the light into the soul— into the heart into one's being. And the other step is to recognize you have a false self. We all have a false self, and that's what we have to let go of. That's the thing that needs transformation and needs cleansing. So I only ask that you begin with letting go of that. That you let your mind and you let all of that old self sink down into the light that you've called. And so then you begin to have operating a meeting between the God of light and our psychological material, the things that we carry and in that meeting, I would say Christ will begin to work on the cleansing of your being. You don't do this, you allow Christ to do it. So I would take that direction. That God must be called—to call Christ. It's like our freedom is so important to the divine. He's not going to in a sense, overwhelm us. But if you called, that's what Christ said, "I'll be with you always." So I would put some emphasis on that beginning this path and being on it, because of what Christ brought from the light into the world—the afterworld, it doesn't demand that you're really sophisticated, knowledgeable or whatever, just that you're a human being and that you're willing to turn—in a sense, making the first turn toward the light.

203

AV: And engage in this—in a regular way.

RF: Yes, to spend some time doing this every day.

AV: Exactly.

RF: Yes, yes, absolutely crucial because then it's just like a plant under the ground that's watered and it gradually becomes stronger and stronger through daily use—the daily practice, so it does ask you to do a daily practice. And if you don't, well then—you just do it now and then, you're not going to get much stronger of course. It's just like working out. So in a way, this is truly a labor, which is what it's been called—labor of the vineyard, or labor of the soul, and hesychastic tradition. And you have to labor some every day.

AV: And at some point during this process, you're going to come up against some difficulties—some things that you've dealt with or that you've experienced in the past or as you referred to, the things that you carry, and how do you deal with those things as they come up?

RF: I think two-fold: I might talk with a beginner about how basically your soul is a *contrarium*. It has a light side and the shadow or dark side. And the light side has all of that potential that wants to come forward and be realized. The other side is the side is in need of cleansing and what the light will do—it will strike both sides of the *contrarium* of the soul simultaneously. So yes, you should expect that the things you carry are going to be activated. But not to mess with you, but for the process of cleansing them, so it might be kind of scary to see them activated, which it is, but what they're really trying to do is help you so you're becoming more and more aware of them and that this is what I need to go into cleansing—this is what needs to be cleansed in me. And on the other side, you will receive promptings from the light, in the light side, about how to live your life in moral and true ways.

AV: "True" here means more deeply in the light and who you are in reality, not a social role.

RF: Actualizing your true soul signature.

AV: Could you talk a little bit about the term "signature," because I think many people might not be familiar with that?

RF: I think you could say that a signature really alludes to the fact that each one of us has an immortal personality of our own—our own signature, our own being that is the individual being-ness that wants to become creative and actualize itself. In other words, one of our deepest feelings over time is I'd really like to become more, at least for those who are somewhat aware, that I'd really like to become more of who I sense or believe that I really am. Well, that's your signature's prompting. We want to become our deepest individual because there's an eternalness about that. That's not lost any more than our love is lost. And so it's the essence of an individual calling being—vocation—whatever different words we may use.

AV: It's our deep nature as opposed to our ego or the social faces that we have, some of which were given to us when we're born or by training or education or by different social roles, and what we're talking about in terms of signature is that distinctive deeper dimension that we can manifest and that's the manifestation of who we really are meant to be. That's the term—which comes from Böhme, "signature."

RF: Yes, in one of the books, *The Signature of All Things*, he alludes to us each having our own signature, which is undeniable if you're really any kind of student of life at all. Why do people leave meaningless jobs? Because so often they're saying I just didn't feel that it had anything to do with who I am.

AV: I think it's important to realize regarding what we've been talking about is that it's a process of flourishing and of becoming who we're meant to be in the sense of how we can flourish. The process here is not erasing the self or erasing who we are or erasing the world around us or however you want to put it. It's developing in a deeper and more profound way, going beyond the burdens that we carry in order to ultimately—to lay down and to see transformed those traumas of the past so that ultimately, we can become who we are in this world. And in the next world, because this world and the next world are not separate.

RF: No. They are not at all, and especially they are very much the same and the important things in this world are the important things in that world. And for us to become who we truly are, that's just the joy to this whole—because in life there are only two things that are essential: a fully realized signature, and a deep love relationship. That's why relationships a lot of times can fail if both people are not involving and helping each other on the path of becoming who they are. It's the other side of love. It's the development of each other's individuality. So we're meant to both develop the love and ultimately develop our signature and they're both eternal.

AV: And part of that process is reflected back in terms of dreams and in terms of course intuition. But dreams are a key to understanding what's happening on a deeper level.

RF: Yes, I think dreams most often will either tell you or give you some kind of information about let's say the shadow side of things—about what's going on and what you need to deal with and things like that and then the other side of the dreams is most often about your need to potentialize yourself—things that you're being called to develop, or continue to unfold.

AV: I think there's another aspect as well, which of course is the latter in the sense of development, but it goes beyond the individual. There is a Tibetan teacher who said that dreams are the United Nations of the mind, meaning that in dreams you can encounter beings—all kind of beings— sometimes of course we interpret these experiences in relation to ourselves or our own consciousness.

RF: Yes, which is both archetypical and individual.

AV: Right. What I'm suggesting is that there is another dimension, which is beyond us as individuals. Of course, we as individuals observe it or we experience it, but then what is beyond us sometimes we're experiencing it or observing it and it's greater than us and beyond us. We can refer to some of it as the archetypical or the collective consciousness, which of course I prefer to Jung's "unconscious," because what I'm referring to here transcends individual consciousness to some extent. So there's this other aspect of what's possible in dream and vision, which goes beyond us and our individual development and you could say it has to do with humanity as a whole, or it's beyond the individual. Revelations of angels and other beings, Gods—there is a long history of this in humanity and so I just wanted to bring that in as another aspect of what we're talking about.

RF: Yes, we're all on the same journey. It's like what you're saying: in some way a universal spiritual dimension is common to all humanity. And—that wants to take us in that direction, reveal the great secrets of itself. So just like you're saying, you might have someone who has a vision in one country centuries ago, and someone who doesn't even know about that person and has a very similar vision about things, because there are those eternal spiritual realities that human beings are imbued with and that want to take us towards those realizations.

AV: That's true and it connects with something that we've talked about before, which is that ultimately what's true is true intrinsically and by that, I mean what is true is true for all of us. And accessible to us as humans by virtue of being human and I think that's important to say because we live in a time in which many people want to deny that and—want to deny the universality of truth. And I think that actually is a key to understanding many things and the mere fact that so many people are denying it does not change it one iota. Why? Because that's the nature of truth.

RF: That's right. It doesn't make any difference what kind of crazy ideas one may have about it, it exists independently of your mental perceptions. So you may not believe a lot of things but that doesn't mean that they're not real or true.

AV: And I wanted to bring that up toward the close of our conversation because I think it's a vital aspect of what informs our conversation as a whole. The kinds of experiences and the kind of process that we're talking about is accessible to us by virtue of being human beings and if someone has heard what we're saying and listened to it, that means that some part of you is waking up or has started to recognize this and if not, as Böhme says, that's okay. Just drop it. Pay no attention to it. And walk away. But if some part of you resonates with it, then that's an indication that this is something for which you feel a calling and that's an extremely important sign that I think you might want to heed.

RF: I absolutely agree. I think that's an indication that you're one of the seekers. And that you're starting to awaken and begin this universal spiritual journey that all human beings are really called to. Of course, you might be quite blind or you don't even have an impulse toward it—you can't get through or you won't let it through—but all the same, there are a lot of people where it's still wanting to get through because it's too deep, it's too universal. It's not going to be denied ultimately. A lot of the modern things that people think are so great, those are the things that are going to fall apart. The things that you and I are talking about aren't going to die; they might be eclipsed for a while, but they're not going to die away.

AV: No, they cannot.

RF: They cannot. It's not the nature—I'd say it's not the nature of the true.

AV: That's an excellent place I think to end.

RF: Yes. Yes.

CPSIA information can be obtained
at www.ICGtesting.com
Printed in the USA
LVHW082315230521
688301LV00005B/247